[illegible]
Con gran ap[illegible]

y colega. Espero que este libro sirva para entender esta especial institución que es el BID.

A Long and Winding Road

The Creation of the Inter-American Development Bank

Un abrazo

[illegible]

A Long and Winding Road

The Creation of the Inter-American
Development Bank

Eugenio Díaz-Bonilla

and

María Victoria del Campo

Contents

Acknowledgments by Eugenio Díaz-Bonilla.......................... vii

Prologue ix

Introduction... xi

First Phase: The International American Bank

a) Early Ideas.. 1

b) The First Pan-American Conference 1889-1890 and the
International American Bank 4

c) Other Economic Issues 9

Second Phase: Trade, Financial, and Exchange Rate Issues

a) Trade and Debt Issues....................................... 13

b) The Federal Reserve and the Expansion of the U.S. Banks 16

c) Exchange Rates and the First World War....................... 17

d) The Credit Binge of the 1920s 21

**Third Phase: The Great Depression, World War II, and the
Inter-American Bank.**

a) The Great Depression and Early Regional Responses 25

b) The Roosevelt Administration, the "Good Neighbor" Policy,
and the Evolution of Regional Financial Issues................. 26

c) The Inter-American Bank.................................... 32

d) Structure and Operations of the Inter-American Bank (I-AB) 34

e) The "Super Bank" that Wasn't.............................. 38

f) The Inter-American Bank and the Creation of the Bretton
Woods Institutions 41

Fourth Phase: The Cold War and the Inter-American Development Bank

a) The Cold War in Latin America and the Early Predominance of Security Approaches 47

b) The Slow Reemergence of the Idea of a Regional Bank: the Quitandinha, Santiago, and Buenos Aires Meetings 55

c) Nixon's Trip in 1958: A Wake-up Call for Hemispheric Cooperation 65

d) The Creation of the Inter-American Development Bank 70

e) The Bogotá Act, the Alliance for Progress, and the Launching of the Bank 77

Understanding the Past, Thinking about the Future

a) International Politics and Democracy 83

Historical Perspectives 83

Current and Future Challenges 86

b) Economic Issues: Finances and Trade 89

Historical Perspectives: Financial Issues 89

Historical Perspectives: Trade and Integration Issues 93

Current and Future Challenges 96

c) International Structures and Governance: Resources 101

Historical Perspectives 101

Current and Future Challenges 106

d) International Structures and Governance: Dialogue, Learning, and Consensus 109

Historical Perspectives 109

Current and Future Challenges 115

Bibliography 119

Index 129

Acknowledgments by Eugenio Díaz-Bonilla

"Te Deum laudamus"

I want to thank Enrique Iglesias, former president of the Inter-American Development Bank (IDB), for his detailed comments on previous drafts of this book and for accepting to write the Prologue. His wisdom is invaluable as is his friendship. This book has also benefitted enormously from the historical work done by Xavier Comas and from his comments on earlier manuscripts. My thanks also go to him. The knowledgeable and dedicated people at the Felipe Herrera Library and at the Legal Library at the IDB have been very helpful as well. My colleagues from the Office of Argentina and Haiti at the IDB (Martín Bes, Ericq Pierre, Miriam Centurion, Marina Simian, María Fernández Moujan, Victoria Cabo, Delenise Lettieri, and Juan Ron) were extremely supportive during the long process of preparation of this book. In particular, Martín provided many insightful suggestions, as usual. Juan and Marina helped with the editing, as did Victoria Díaz-Bonilla, my youngest daughter. I appreciate the comments by Héctor Luisi to an earlier version of this book.

Of course, they are not responsible for possible errors and omissions, and for garbled sentences. Also, the interpretations and opinions are those of the authors and should not be attributed to the IDB or its member countries and governments.

I want to recognize the Elliot School of International Affairs of the George Washington University that gave me the opportunity to teach a short course on the IDB during several semesters. Preparing for the lectures and the interaction with my students allowed me to delve deeper into the fascinating history of this institution.

My love and gratitude to my wife Graciela: many weekends were stolen from her trying to finish this book. My debt to her and the rest of my family, however, greatly exceeds those lost hours.

The book is mainly dedicated to the employees of the IDB: past, present, and future. We should never forget that this institution reflects the hopes, dreams, and efforts of countless people over many decades.

Working at the IDB is a privilege and a great responsibility, which should be humbling. It is not a 9AM-5PM job. The IDB must serve the people in the region, particularly the poor and vulnerable, who in a real way pay the salaries and expenditures of the Bank. The aspirations of the people of Latin America and the Caribbean to build societies with modern economic structures, decent jobs, democratic participation, solidarity and equity, and sustainable use of energy and natural resources, require that the Bank always be a relevant and dedicated partner.

Our hope as authors is that a better knowledge of the history of this remarkable institution will help reinforce the spirit of service in all of us, so we never forget those for whom we must work every day.

Prologue

In my farewell speech as president of IDB, in September 2005, I pointed out that in order to examine the challenges that the region and the Bank face we need to ask: "where do we come from?" It is always necessary to look back first to evaluate where we are heading to and, especially, where we ought to go, in order to preserve the relevance of the institution and to make the Bank the great ally and partner of our countries in the constant fight for economic and social development.

This book addresses the question of where the IDB comes from with a comprehensive historical narrative that begins in the nineteenth century: since then, the hopes and dreams of the peoples of the region for the construction of more developed societies had the idea of a regional bank as a central component.

My own experience as president of the Bank made me aware that the IDB operates in a context influenced by the convergence of at least three forces. The first one comes from world development, which we certainly do not control, and sometimes takes us by surprise. The second one is the evolution of the ideas, which are crucial to organize our understanding of reality, but that, at the same time, are also flowing and updating every day. And lastly, we must consider global politics, particularly reflected on sometimes difficult political relations between United States and Latin America, or some of its countries, that inevitably reflect on the relations between the United States and the Bank. The conciliation of these three forces has always made the task of managing the Bank very complex.

This book highlights the fact that a similar framework was also central to the process of creation of the IDB. After many failed attempts, the Bank was created in 1959 when different factors in global economic and political developments, and in the realm of the ideas, converged in the dialogue between Latin America and the Caribbean and the United States, later expanded to Canada and countries outside the region, in Europe and Asia.

The result of this long dialogue has been a fundamentally Latin American and Caribbean institution which is at the same time truly global, and which possesses great assets: an enviable financial strength; the trust of its member countries, based on the sense of ownership; and a model of decision-making built around consensus that produces solid and sustainable decisions and that has developed a culture of solidarity by defending from the beginning the participation and rights of the smaller and more vulnerable countries. It is an institution that has been side-by-side with the member countries in good and bad times, being always a constructive support to their relations with U.S. Administrations and international organizations in Washington; that has contributed to the knowledge of the economic, social and political problems of the region; that has always opened spaces for a frank and cooperative dialogue with governments, political groups, private sector and the civil society; that has respected the sovereignty and culture of its member countries; and that has tried to develop topics of high spiritual value and ethical content.

The historical narrative presented in this book should remind everyone interested in Latin America and the Caribbean of the long historical quest in search of economic, social, and political development in the region. In particular, this work should also be an important piece of reading for IDB staff. The Bank has qualified staff that shares a vocation of service. These are people that work at the Bank, above all, for the immense opportunity that comes from dedicating themselves to a great cause.

The historical perspective of this book should reinforce the conviction of belonging to a special institution: working for the IDB is a privilege and a vast responsibility, not only with the poor and vulnerable people in the region, but also with the thousands of hard-working visionaries that turned this institution into a reality, into something that, as Felipe Herrera always reminded us, is "more than a bank."

Enrique Iglesias
Secretary of the "Secretaría General Iberoamericana" (SEGIB) and former president of the Inter-American Development Bank (1988-2005)

Introduction

At the 1964 annual meeting of the Inter-American Development Bank (IDB)[1] in Panama, Felipe Herrera, then the president of the Bank, declared that "our institution must continue to demonstrate that, being a bank, it is also more than a bank...." (Time Magazine, April 24, 1964). "Being more than a bank" was Herrera's signature phrase for referring to the IDB. The same Time article noted that "Latin Americans call it 'el BID' or simply 'our bank'.... Latin Americans had the original idea, have their own man in charge, and put up more than half of the initial $813 million capital."

It was clear that the United States supported the institution because at that same meeting Douglas Dillon, then Secretary of the Treasury, pledged to increase U.S. contributions to the IDB by 750 million dollars (about 5,300 million dollars measured in March 2010 values) over the following three years.

What is this institution that after Herrera many have claimed it is "more than a bank," and how did it come into existence?

The IDB is the oldest and largest regional development bank and it has served as a model for other similar institutions that were subsequently created. During the 1990s, the IDB became the main source of multilateral financing for economic, social, and institutional development projects as well as trade and regional integration programs in Latin America and the Caribbean (LAC), overtaking the World Bank and other international financial organizations operating in the region.[2] A crucial institutional feature, noted in the Time article, is that the Latin American countries (i.e. the borrowers at the IDB) have contributed a majority of the capital of the Bank, which, during the debates about its creation, led its critics to dismiss it as the "debtors' bank." That part of IDB's history is relatively well known.

---

[1] In this book we will use the long title as well as the shorter references "IDB" or "the Bank" (with capital letter) to refer to the Inter-American Development Bank.
[2] When referring to Latin America and the Caribbean we may use indistinctively "Latin America," "LAC," and/or "the region."

Less known is the fact that although the IDB was formally established in 1959, the long and complex historical journey leading to its creation started during the nineteenth century. Now that the IDB has passed the threshold of fifty years since its formal creation, it may be an appropriate time to take a closer look at the long historical process that gave birth to this remarkable institution.

History shows that the evolution of the idea of a regional bank and, finally, the creation of the IDB, cannot be separated from the state of the relations between Latin America and the United States. At times, those interactions have been contentious and antagonistic. However, they have also experienced sustained periods of convergence of interests and building of consensus. When "latinos" and "gringos" were able to articulate their interests into convergent visions, the IDB was first created and later thrived; when they were at odds, the idea of a bank did not materialize, or, after the institution came into existence, its functioning was under strain.

The history of the creation of the IDB narrated in the next chapters shows, within a specific institutional narrative, several of the main traits of the U.S. foreign policy in that country's rise to become a global power. It also highlights Latin America's attempts to engage and interact with its prominent neighbor in ways that supported the region's own aspirations to political independence and economic and social progress.

In this regard, the first point to be noticed is that the ups and downs of the notion of a regional bank were deeply intertwined with the persistent U.S. effort to keep foreign (mainly European) influences out of Latin America and the Caribbean. As articulated by U.S. policy makers over the years, this quest has had security, political, and economic components (Smith, 1996). In terms of security, the United States tried to block external military powers from meddling in the region. The political aspects included the opposition to forms of government based on monarchical, national-socialist, fascist, and communist principles. Regarding economic aspects, the United States tried to expand its external trade, investment, and financial connections in the region, mainly through fostering a friendly business climate for its private sector. Successive U.S. governments usually considered that this expansion of its private sector was also the best way to support economic progress in the region.

These aims, though not always compatible (such as when security concerns led the United States to tolerate or even support authoritarian regimes in the region), were combined in different ways during the nineteenth and twentieth century, providing the framework for the evolution of the different proposals for an inter-American financial institution.

For Latin American countries, one of the objectives was to limit U.S. security and political aims from affecting their political and territorial sovereignty. But those countries also wanted to maintain the United States engaged in the region, at times even invoking the Monroe Doctrine to refocus U.S. attention to the region. In the economic arena, Latin America usually tried to maintain U.S. involvement in regional trade and finance while searching for more balanced commercial and financial relations --not an easy task considering the differences in economic size evident since the early nineteenth century.[3] In other words, Latin America had to manage the double objective of maintaining the United States engaged in the region while reducing the power asymmetries with the weaker neighbors through multilateral legal structures and institutions. From a Latin American perspective, the undesirable extremes would have been an overbearing involvement of the United States in the region, or a United States that ignored its regional neighbors and shifted its security, political, and economic interests elsewhere.

Therefore, in terms of the regional bank, the main goal of Latin America has been to create a multilateral lending institution with U.S. participation, but which was, at the same time, responsive to the region's needs and aspirations.

A second theme highlighted by the narrative is that the evolution of the proposals for a regional financial institution was heavily influenced by the socio-economic and political developments in the region. Market fluctuations shaped Latin American demands for a financial institution and its services, with periods of falling export prices and volatile capital flows leading to more urgent requests for

---

[3] According to historical data collected by Angus Maddison (2003) in late nineteenth century and early twentieth century, the eight LAC countries with longest series of recorded economic data (Argentina, Brazil, Chile, Colombia, Mexico, Peru, Uruguay, and Venezuela) and that accounted for about 85 percent of total GDP of the region, represented only 20 percent of the U.S. GDP measured in PPP equivalent dollars. In 1959, at the time when the IDB was finally created, the same eight countries had reached about 28 percent of the U.S. GDP (and all LAC countries about 32 percent). Using the same data base, in the 2000s those eight LAC countries were about 34 percent of the U.S. GDP, and all LAC countries, around 39 percent.

such an institution. This pattern continued after the creation of the Bank, whose operation and use of resources was influenced by the social and economic changes in the region. In political terms, the best times of the IDB were when democratic governments in the region, through the participatory structure of governance of the institution, transmitted the will of the people to the strategies and operations of the Bank.

A third topic in the Bank's history is the less noticed fact that the United States and Latin American countries developed a significant corpus of diplomatic experience in the construction of international arrangements through the interaction and exchange of ideas about appropriate rules and institutions in the region. In those interactions, LAC intellectuals and policy makers were able to influence, although in different degrees, the final shape of regional policies and institutions. This should be less surprising once it is realized that, as noted by Dominguez (2007), the Americas have one of the longest traditions of international cooperation in the world. The United States later extrapolated those regional experiences to the global arena once that country became the dominant international actor after World War II. An example discussed in this book is how the Inter-American Bank of 1940 served as a precedent for the International Monetary Fund (IMF) and the World Bank (see Horsefield, J. K. 1969; Bordo and Schwartz, 2001; and Helleiner, 2006).

Those three themes will reappear in the following chapters on the history of the creation of the IDB. Within that narrative, four distinct periods can be identified.

The first phase started during the period of independence and national consolidation of the Latin republics in the nineteenth century and ended after the First Pan-American Conference (October 1889-April 1890). During that conference, an International American Bank (IAB) was proposed, but the enabling legislation was defeated in the U.S. Congress some years later.

After that, there is a second period of about four decades when different ideas for regional financial cooperation were floated, but these attempts faded with the pain and disruption of World War I and the Great Depression of the 1930s.

The third phase started with the "Good Neighbor" policy during the Presidency of Franklin Delano Roosevelt and led to the proposal for the creation of the Inter-American Bank (I-AB) in 1940. The treaty was negotiated and signed by the United States and thirteen other countries from Latin America and the Caribbean. However, the request for approval of the bank's charter languished in the U.S. Congress for several years, until finally the Truman Administration withdrew it from consideration in 1947.

The fourth phase, leading finally to the creation of the Inter-American Development Bank in 1959, was part of the reevaluation of U.S. policy towards Latin America by the Eisenhower Administration in the context of the Cold War, which in part prefigured Kennedy's "Alliance for Progress." The successful start and quick consolidation of the IDB was closely related to the combined work of the United States and Latin American countries around the ideals of the Alliance.

We utilized mostly changes in U.S. policies to punctuate those phases because of two reasons. First, in Latin America there was a more permanent and widespread (but not unanimous) support for the creation of a strong financial institution to promote the economic progress of the region, while the interest for such institution in the United States fluctuated. Therefore, a change in the U.S. position is what usually signaled the passage from one phase to the next. Second, and although there were some voices calling for an exclusively Latin American institution as early as the mid nineteenth century, the economic importance of the U.S. presence for the creation of a strong regional bank was obvious to most Latin American policy makers. It should be emphasized, however, that although the different periods are here identified with changes in U.S. policies, this does not detract from the fact that the contributions of Latin American thinking to the creation of a regional financial institution have been very significant, as the following chapters will show. At the same time, a detailed history of policy changes regarding such institution *within* Latin American countries (which are certainly not homogeneous) greatly exceeds the scope of this book.

Each of the four phases will be analyzed in a separate chapter.

After that, the last chapter highlights some enduring aspects of the relations between Latin America and the United States that emerge from the historical narrative about the creation of the IDB. Based on those considerations about the pre-history of the Bank, we try to interpret some aspects of its evolution since 1959 and we also speculate about possible forces and issues that may shape its future.

We believe that a deeper understanding of the emergence and evolution of the IDB can contribute to building better and more participatory structures of international governance and global policy making --a crucial topic highlighted by the debates of the Group of twenty (G-20) countries.[4]

---

[4] The G-20 was established in 1999 to bring together Finance Ministers and Central Bank Governors of some key industrialized and developing economies to discuss systemic global economic issues. The members include nineteen countries (Argentina, Australia, Brazil, Canada, China, France, Germany, India, Indonesia, Italy, Japan, Mexico, Russia, Saudi Arabia, South Africa, Republic of Korea, Turkey, United Kingdom, and the United States) and the European Union. Other countries and international institutions are also invited to the meetings. Since 2008, and with the objective of dealing with the problems posed by the recent global financial crisis, the Heads of State of the G-20 group have participated in the meetings.

First Phase

The International American Bank

a) Early Ideas

The evolution of the idea of a bank for the Americas must be seen in the context of the triangle of international relations between the United States, the European powers, and Latin American countries.

During the early nineteenth century Latin countries made several attempts at strengthening Pan-Americanism in a series of regional conferences: Panama (1826), Lima (1847), Santiago (1856), and Lima (1864). The main objective was to protect their newly acquired independence from external encroachment. Therefore, those conferences focused mostly on military and defense issues. However, the participants also acknowledged the need for economic cooperation among the countries that had emerged from their common struggle against colonial rule. For instance, in the first congress held in Panama City in 1826, Simón Bolívar's main objective was the establishment of a system of collective security, but the proposed agenda also called for the negotiation of treaties of commerce and navigation (Inman, 1965; Maisch, 2004).

There were also other voices calling for greater regional economic cooperation. A case in point was Juan Bautista Alberdi, an Argentine lawyer that would later be the main inspiration behind the 1853 Argentine Constitution. In 1844 he wrote a pamphlet about the "Convenience and Objective of a General American Congress" that was widely circulated at that time. Alberdi argued that the Latin republics should focus less on military and political issues and dedicate their attention to the collective solution of the challenges of economic modernization. He suggested the need for regional economic integration, including the establishment of a commercial customs union, a common currency, and a Continental Bank to finance the economic progress of the American republics (Alberdi, 1844 and

1886; Maisch, 2004). His proposals, however, did not consider the inclusion of the United States.[5]

At the 1864 Congress in Lima, Peru (the second in that city), Argentina, Chile, Colombia, El Salvador, Guatemala, Peru, and Venezuela signed a treaty about their collective security, but those countries also worked on other multilateral treaties covering trade and navigation issues (Inman 1965, Maisch, 2004).

In the United States the ideas about the importance and potential expansion of inter-American ties also evolved over time. In his farewell speech, President George Washington warned against "entangling alliances" with Europe (the "Old World"); but he expected external commercial ties to expand, particularly in the "New World" of the Americas (Washington, 1796). In 1808, Thomas Jefferson also stressed the importance of working together with the Latin republics for the common interest of the Americas (Inman, 1965). Henry Clay told the U.S. Congress in 1817 that the United States should support the independence of South America, considering that "they would obey the laws of the system of the New World... in contradiction to that of Europe" (Inman, 1965). Later in 1823, the Monroe Doctrine, originally aimed at limiting Russian expansion in the northwest of the United States, stated the U.S. objective of keeping European powers from meddling in the Americas. In this continent the new states were expected to remain independent and maintain republican governments.

In the following decades inter-American ties were deeply strained by the unfolding of the doctrine of Manifest Destiny, backed by what was called "pocketbook diplomacy" and military campaigns (Smith, 1996). The Mexican War (1846-48) expanded significantly the U.S. territory and caused strong alarm among Latin American nations. The U.S. Civil War (1861–1865) generated a pause in that territorial expansion. But once the effects of the war faded away and the evolution of U.S. industry underscored the need for expanded external markets, the establishment of an economic area of influence with the Southern republics emerged as an attractive alternative to territorial imperialism.[6] The need for export markets led to an active

---

[5] A "customs union" is an association of nations to promote free trade among the members, maintaining a common set of tariffs for nations that are not members. The difference with a free trade agreement is that in the latter case member countries do not have a common external tariff.

[6] The creation of a sphere of interest through political and economic ties with the countries to the South was considered both less burdensome than territorial

international economic policy, with the Department of State expected to represent U.S. private interests abroad. A major challenge for those interests was Europe's presence in the Caribbean and its privileged commercial position in South America.

The inauguration of President James Garfield in March 1881, with James Blaine as his Secretary of State, initiated a period of intensified U.S. interest in Latin America. Previously, as a Congressman, James Garfield had focused on three themes related to foreign policy: the importance of Latin American, and other non-European, countries in U.S. international relations; the rejection of territorial expansion; and arbitration as the solution to international grievances (Peskin, 1979). Blaine was also convinced that the United States should play a more active role in hemispheric affairs. His immediate concern appears to have been a series of bilateral conflicts affecting Latin American countries in the early 1880s.[7] Blaine, and also President Garfield, felt that the United States had to intercede to limit the spread of military conflict, thus reducing the possibility of European intervention (ideas that anticipated Theodore Roosevelt's Doctrine) (Peskin, 1979).[8]

To implement these ideas Blaine actively campaigned for the idea of a Pan-American conference. The meeting was going to be held in Panama by late 1882. He had very high hopes: as Blaine explained to Garfield, the conference "will bring us into kindly relations with all the American nations. It will promote the reign of law and order. It will increase production and consumption.... It will, at all events, be a

---

imperialism and easier to justify morally. Moreover, there were also some arguments based on racial prejudices that considered the annexation of territories with a different demographic composition as potentially disruptive for the political and social system of the United States (Smith, 1996).

[7] There were bilateral problems over territorial issues between Mexico and Guatemala; Cost Rica and Colombia; Argentina and Chile; and the latter country against Bolivia and Peru. At about the same time, France was threatening to intervene in Venezuela to collect unpaid debts.

[8] As Peskin argues "In Blaine's hands the Monroe Doctrine became something more than the traditional warning to Europe to stay on its side of the ocean. It was addressed to the other American states as well. Inter-American wars and disputes would no longer be allowed to threaten territorial boundaries which were henceforth to be regarded as immutable. The Doctrine, in short, would not only protect American states from Europe but also from each other." The method would be arbitration, "hoping that peaceful negotiations, under the paternal direction of the United States, could replace the endemic outbreaks of inter-American warfare" (Peskin, 1979).

friendly and auspicious beginning in the direction of American influence and trade in a large field which we have hitherto neglected" (cited in Peskin, 1979). However, planning for the conference ended with the shooting of President Garfield in July of 1881 and his death in September of that year, about six months after his inauguration.

His successor, President Chester Arthur, suspended the Pan-American Conference and Blaine left the cabinet in December 1881. For several years after Garfield's assassination the conference was postponed by political disagreements in the United States. Historians differ on the motives behind Blaine's hemispheric objectives. Blaine himself always presented economic reasons for his interest in the Latin republics (Peskin, 1979). Commercial integration served the United States well, as new markets were crucial for its economy. But the fear that political and military tensions would attract external interventions also played a role. In any case, both economic and military objectives converged into Blaine's belief that greater commercial interdependence would eventually bring stability and peace to the Southern nations. A customs union giving preference to inter-American trade would, in Blaine's opinion, reduce the likelihood that "the United States would have to defend the Monroe Doctrine" (Peskin, 1979). Blaine would try again those ideas with a new U.S. president in 1889.

b) The First Pan-American Conference 1889-1890 and the International American Bank

In March 1889, Benjamin Harrison took office as the twenty-third president of the United States. Blaine, who had supported him in the Republican primary, was appointed Secretary of State and began to promote again the idea of a Pan-American Conference. Latin American republics did not react immediately to the invitation to participate in the conference, and there were some doubts in the U.S. government as to how many countries would finally accept. In the end, all came except the Dominican Republic.[9]

In October 1889 the First Pan-American Conference started in Washington D.C. It was a long event that ended several months later in April 1890. As mentioned, James Blaine wanted to expand trade and

---

[9] In addition to the United States, the participating nations included Argentina, Brazil, Bolivia, Chile, Colombia, Costa Rica, Ecuador, El Salvador, Guatemala, Haiti, Honduras, Mexico, Nicaragua, Paraguay, Peru, Uruguay, and Venezuela.

financial integration towards the South. He was concerned that the United States, while having strong economic ties with Mexico, the Caribbean and Central America, had a small presence in South America, where mainly the United Kingdom, but also other European powers, held dominant economic positions. Therefore, Blaine presented the participants with an ambitious economic agenda: the creation of a customs union in the Americas; free navigation of rivers; harmonized customs regulations, port duties, sanitary regulations, weights and measures, and patents and trade-marks; investment in an intercontinental railway; the establishment of a monetary union with a common currency; and the creation of a regional bank, among other things (Comas, 2000). The agenda was similar in many aspects to the one presented by Alberdi fifty years before, but now the United States was the convening party and a central player of the continental program.

The different topics were assigned to separate groups of delegates, organized in committees. The Committee on Banking discussed the proposal for the creation of a regional bank. This idea irked some of the Latin American delegates: the Chilean representative, for example, was, initially, a vocal opponent of the measure. He claimed that the main barriers to commercial expansion between the United States and Latin America were trade protectionism and lack of transportation; that "banks do not create commerce;" and that existing banks in Latin America could perform the functions assigned to the branches of the planned regional bank. In the end, however, the Chilean delegate joined the consensus and the proposal for a regional bank was approved by all fourteen delegates in that committee. The report arguing for the creation of the bank was sent to the plenary of the conference on April 8, 1890.[10]

The report recommended the chartering of an International American Bank, a *private* entity with branches in the different countries that adhered to the proposal.[11] The report argued that "the future of the commercial relations between North, South and Central America" depended on "the complete and prompt development of

---

[10] The countries represented in the committee were Argentina, Brazil, Bolivia, Chile, Colombia, Costa Rica, Guatemala, Honduras, Mexico, Nicaragua, Paraguay, Peru, United States and Venezuela. Around the time of the Conference, the 1890 Baring crisis started in Argentina, weakening London, which may have also had an influence on the deliberations.

[11] The following quotes are from "International American Conference (1st: 1889-90: Washington, D C.) Volume: 2." Pages 829-875

international banking facilities." The importance of transportation facilities was also recognized, but the latter would generate only partial benefits when "compared with the benefits which might be derived were the two improvements to progress together."

The report criticized "the large amount of commissions now paid to the European bankers." Those commissions could not only be decreased, but "would be paid to American bankers or merchants themselves, and in this way a share of the profits...could be kept in the financial centers of this continent."[12] It was also noted that there were neither direct trade credit facilities nor long-term financing between United States and Latin America: therefore "manufacturers and merchants at distant points" could not establish commercial relations except through "the intervention of European banks and bankers, which are not interested in the extension of trade between the different countries represented in this conference except in a secondary and subordinate sense."

The report further argued that the United States had the capital to help create such a banking entity, but that currently it was impossible to do so "without some change in the legislation of the United States to secure a sufficient aggregation of capital in corporate form, and so free from the burdensome restraints and taxes now imposed upon moneyed corporations as to permit competition on equal terms with the European bankers." The report noted that there was "no general statute of the United States nor of any of the States of the United States under which a banking company can be organized with ample capital, which would have the power of issuing such letters of credit and transacting such business as is done by the leading banking companies of London."

Therefore, the committee proposed the passage of a law by the United States incorporating the International American Bank, "with ample capital, and in which citizens of the several countries in the conference could buy shares 'pro rata' to their foreign commerce." The bank could not create money (something that the U.S. chartered banks at that time could do); but it would have all other powers of commercial and investment banks (such as receiving deposits, issuing letters of credit, making loans, buying and selling bills of exchange, issuing guaranties, and so on).

---

[12] The word "American" was used, as it should, in a general sense that included all countries in the Americas (North, Central, and South).

The committee's report also argued that the proposed bank could help the governments in the Americas to place foreign loans and "all classes of State and municipal securities" in financial markets, thus reducing the dependence of Latin American governments on European banks. It would also offer Latin American investors the possibility to invest in "all classes of North American securities," while the investors of the United States would be able to invest "in all classes of securities issued by the States, municipalities, or corporations of Latin America."

The report also proposed the establishment of branches or agencies in all of the principal financial centers of the Americas, "with the formal recognition of the Governments of the several States in which such agencies are established."

The arguments for the creation of the International American Bank included a prescient statement that would come true about a quarter century later: "while the sentiments of the independent nations of this continent are favorable to the settlement of all disputes by arbitration as expressed by resolutions introduced in this Conference, thus rendering war highly improbable if not impossible among them, there exists no such guaranty that war may not take place in Europe;" and, if that happened, there would be "financial disaster and distress" in the Americas.

The participation of the U.S. government would take place through the chartering and close supervision of the institution in the United States. No money from the U.S. government was involved, and the bank, as previously mentioned, would not be allowed to create money (banking notes). This was a crucial issue in the United States, given that the creation of the Federal Reserve, which would centralize the money supply, was still twenty years away. The importance of having the official U.S. support was that "the establishment of an international bank by authority of Congress would promptly command from the other American Governments concurrent legislation."

The conference approved the proposal on April 14, 1890, recommending "to the Governments here represented the granting of liberal concessions to facilitate inter-American banking, and especially such as may be necessary for the establishment of an International American Bank, with branches or agencies in the several countries represented in this Conference."

After the conclusion of the conference, in May 1890, Blaine transmitted the resolution to President Harrison with a request to the U.S. Congress to provide a charter for the International American

Bank. Blaine referred to the costs (that he equated to a "tax") of channeling the transactions through London, and emphasized the importance of approving a U.S. law incorporating such a bank. President Harrison promptly sent the resolution and letter from Blaine to Congress for appropriate action, noting that the financial institution proposed did not involve costs for the government. He argued that the legislation was needed to give the proposed bank a corporate franchise and "to promote public confidence by requiring that its condition and transactions shall be submitted to a scrutiny similar to that which is now exercised over our domestic banking system."

The issue was discussed for several years, starting with the fifty-first U.S. Congress in 1890. The lawmakers supporting the measure used many of the arguments of the report (such as that trade between United States and Latin countries had to go through banks in London, which charged high commissions and delayed the process); but they also expanded on several other topics, particularly the possibility of displacing the United Kingdom and also other European countries, such as Germany, as main trade partners for Latin American countries. For instance, Marriott Brosius, a Republican member of the House Committee on Banking and Currency, complained that although the United States was the largest buyer of Latin American products, Great Britain sold the region three dollars worth of goods for every dollar the United States exported (U.S. House of Representatives, 1897). During the debate it was also mentioned the more distant objective of helping New York displace London as the main international financial center.

Opponents argued that the U.S. Congress lacked the power under the U.S. Constitution to create such an institution, which could only be established by the States of the Union. This argument was answered in detail by the supporters of the legislation, anticipating in part some of the debates about the creation of the Federal Reserve in 1913. Others angrily complained against giving such a large financial institution "the exclusive monopoly of the transactions in business and exchange with the countries where it establishes branch banks," when "Congress should not grant a monopoly for private purposes to private individuals" (House of Representatives, 1897, "Views of the Minority" p.2 and p.5). Since the legislation allowed the establishment of branches within the United States, a related concern was that the new bank would displace smaller domestic banks in the individual States (see reports to the House of Representatives for the fifty-first, fifty-second, and fifty-fourth Congresses, in 1890, 1892, and 1897, respectively).

After several years of debates, the legislation came to a vote in December 1898 and it was defeated in the House of Representatives by 148 *nays* to 103 *yeas*. The New York Times, probably reflecting the interest of the city in becoming a major international financial center, editorialized on December 18, 1898 that "the defeat of the International American Bank bill … was a perfectly typical Populist performance, and therefore a valuable triumph for ignorance and prejudice."

The First Pan-American Conference discussed many other issues in addition to the International American Bank. One of Blaine's main objectives was the creation of a customs union for the Americas, but it faced strong resistance from several Southern countries. Countries such as Argentina that had strong links with the United Kingdom, then a greater power and formidable industrial producer, were unconvinced about the advantages of integrating their economies with the United States. There were heated exchanges between Mr. Henderson (one of the principals in the U.S. delegation), and Mr. Sáenz Peña (an Argentine delegate who would later become president of his country), with both accusing the other side of protectionism.

Blaine, however, obtained support from the conference for the negotiation of reciprocal trade treaties and the U.S. government actively pursued this alternative in the following years. The idea of a continental common currency based on silver was also debated. Variations of this proposal, crucial for regional trade and financial operations, reappeared in the next years (see below).

An apparently small item of the Pan-American Conference that later became very relevant was the creation in Washington, D.C. of a Commercial Bureau of the American Republics. This office later became the Pan-American Union (1910) and, finally, the Organization of American States (1948).

All in all, the First Pan-American Conference represented a significant hemispheric effort to find common grounds on a variety of issues that set the hemispheric agenda for many decades.

c) Other Economic Issues

The congressional rejection put an end to the idea of a regional institution with the powers of a commercial and investment bank, and with branches in several U.S. and Latin American cities. The financial avenue to expand U.S. trade with Latin American countries and displace the United Kingdom and other European countries from their preeminent role in the region was closed.[13]   The remaining policy option was the negotiation of reciprocal trade treaties, a peculiar notion in which Latin American countries unwilling to grant commercial benefits to the United States would be subject to *higher* tariffs on their exports.

Blaine pursued this option energetically. In 1891 and 1892 the United States negotiated eight reciprocity agreements with Latin American countries. The two most important were with Brazil and Spain (in the latter case, representing Cuba and Puerto Rico); there were also treaties with the Dominican Republic, Great Britain (for the British West Indies), El Salvador, Guatemala, Nicaragua, and Honduras. Blaine and the Harrison Administration sought agreements with Haiti, Colombia, and Venezuela, but were rejected and then raised tariffs against those countries. Blaine also tried and failed with Mexico, Argentina, Peru, Ecuador, and Denmark (for the Danish West Indies), but did not increase tariffs. The only countries in Latin America and the Caribbean with whom treaties were not pursued were Chile, Uruguay, Paraguay, and Bolivia (Pletcher, 1978).

The idea of a regional financial institution reemerged from time to time in the following decades, but with different characteristics, depending on the issues confronting the United States and the Latin American countries. The International American Bank tried to lift the financial constraint to regional trade imposed by the fact that the charters of the U.S. banks did not grant them the powers to operate internationally -- a restriction that was related to the fragmented nature of national and state regulations.

But there were other issues affecting trade and finances, such as volatility of exchange rates, which were discussed during the First Pan-American Conference. In particular, the United States proposed to stabilize exchange rates using a silver standard in the region (the United States had a bimetallic system based on gold and silver). This proposal was further pursued in a meeting of the International American Monetary Commission, which gathered in Washington, DC, between January 7 and April 4, 1891, at the invitation of the United

---

[13] Although the United States had been steadily growing in importance as a trade partner to the region, it was still behind the United Kingdom. For instance, in 1894, the United Kingdom accounted for over 40 percent of South American imports, while the U.S. provided about 14 percent (see U.S. House of Representatives, 1897).

States.[14] The issue of a common monetary system for the region resurfaced from time to time in the next decades. The proposals ranged from the more ambitious idea of a common currency to the less-demanding notion of stable exchange rates across different currencies based on a U.S. dollar standard. Although these ideas were originally unrelated to the creation of a bank, they evolved later to also encompass the concept of a regional financial institution, as discussed in the next chapters.

---

[14] José Martí, who participated as a delegate in the conference, wrote a strongly critical analysis of the proposal for a continental currency. He argued that it would strain Latin America's links with Europe and would leave the value of the currency to be created at the mercy of the decisions of the U.S. government (Martí, 1891).

Second Phase

Trade, Financial, and Exchange Rate Issues

a) Trade and Debt Issues

Despite its congressional defeat in 1898, the proposal of the International American Bank reappeared in the Second Pan-American Conference held in Mexico between October 1901 and January 1902. In an example of the persistence of topics once they become part of international agendas, the conference ratified the recommendation of creating such an institution and proposed opening branches in New York, Chicago, San Francisco, New Orleans, Buenos Aires, or in "any other important mercantile center" (Comas, 2000). The resolution mentioned that the functioning of the bank would follow the internal legislation of each country but with common rules for the approval of credits and charging commissions. It was argued that such harmonization would facilitate international financial transactions, thus enhancing the development of commercial relations in the region. The resolution was signed by Argentina, Bolivia, Colombia, Costa Rica, the Dominican Republic, Ecuador, El Salvador, Guatemala, Haiti, Honduras, Mexico, Nicaragua, Paraguay, Peru, the United States, and Uruguay (Brazil, Chile, and Venezuela did not sign the resolution).

This was the last attempt regarding the International American Bank. Finally, catching up to the fact that the U.S. Congress had rejected the legislation for such an institution, references to the bank in subsequent Pan-American conferences basically disappeared.

The main issue discussed in Mexico was arbitration and the settlement of controversies arising from pecuniary claims of individuals of one country against the government of another. The delegations recommended that their countries become parties to The Hague Convention of 1899, which provided for voluntary arbitration. At the same time, ten delegations signed a project for a treaty that allowed compulsory arbitration.

The conference also worked on other topics such as extradition of criminals, patents, and copyrights. It was also agreed to reorganize the International Bureau of American Republics, thus continuing the strengthening of the regional institutional machinery that would eventually become the Organization of American States in 1948.

Given the fact that Germany and Great Britain had sent naval forces to Venezuela to collect debts in 1902, the issue of arbitration became increasingly pressing. A consequence of that intervention was that, in 1904, Theodore Roosevelt articulated what was known later as the Roosevelt Corollary to the Monroe Doctrine. According to Roosevelt "if a nation shows that it knows how to act with reasonable efficiency and decency in social and political matters, if it keeps order and pays its obligations, it need fear no interference from the United States." On the other hand, "chronic wrongdoing, or an impotence which results in a general loosening of the ties of civilized society, may ... ultimately require intervention by some civilized nation, and in the Western Hemisphere the adherence of the United States to the Monroe Doctrine may force the United States, however reluctantly, in flagrant cases of such wrongdoing or impotence, to the exercise of an international police power" (Theodore Roosevelt, 1904).

The Roosevelt Corollary proclaimed the principle of noninterference in hemispheric affairs by external actors, while asserting the right of the United States to intervene in case of a breakdown in governance in Latin American countries. A consequence of the Corollary was that the U.S. banks were encouraged to assume the debts of several Latin American and Caribbean countries to prevent the forcible collection of debts by European countries. But, in turn, this approach led to U.S. military interventions and political supervision of some of its weaker neighbors.

Concerned about these developments, Latin American countries looked for remedies during the Third Pan-American Conference (Rio de Janeiro, July–August 1906). Again the issues of arbitration and the compulsory collection of public debts were central topics. Most Latin American countries agreed with the 1902 Drago Doctrine (basically an extension of the previous Calvo Doctrine), which called for a ban on the forcible collection of debts by foreign powers.[15] The general

---

[15] The Argentine Minister of Foreign Affairs Luis María Drago argued in 1902 that no foreign power (including the United States) could use force against an American nation to collect debt. It was based on ideas presented by Carlos Calvo, an Argentine

premise of the Drago Doctrine was that effective arbitration mechanisms would pave the way for growing cooperation in other areas such as trade and investment. Furthermore, it affirmed that the rules for the collection of indemnities should apply equally to all nations and ruled out the use of force to ensure repayment of debts.

At the conference, Secretary of State Elihu Root announced that the United States renounced military intervention to collect debts. The matter was discussed again at the Second International Conference of The Hague, where the United States accepted a resolution condemning the collection of debts by force except when the debtor country refused arbitration (Inman, 1965).

At the Rio Conference there was no specific mention of the creation of a regional bank. However, given some weakening of the monetary systems based on the gold standard, the conference considered recommendations to conduct a study of monetary systems in the different republics. The analysis would look at fluctuations of exchange rates and their impact on trade and industrial development (Comas, 2000). There was also a resolution to create a division of Commerce, Customs, and Commercial Statistics within the Bureau of American Republics to conduct studies on the standardization of customs and consular laws among the American states.

References to a regional financial institution were also absent during the Fourth Pan-American Conference (Buenos Aires, July–August 1910), where an agreement was signed that maintained in force the arbitration treaty that had been approved in the second conference and extended in Rio de Janeiro in 1906. In an important development the commercial office started by the First Pan-American Conference was given new functions. They included, among other things, compiling and distributing economic statistics, collecting treaties and conventions, and, crucially, acting as a permanent commission of the Inter-American Conferences with an expanded role in the organization of those events and in the follow-up activities. The original office was renamed the Bureau of the Pan-American Union.

---

lawyer, whose writings had argued that jurisdiction in international investment disputes lies with the country in which the investment is located (i.e. a foreign investor must use local courts instead of those in his home country).

b) The Federal Reserve and the Expansion of the U.S. Banks

In March 1913, Woodrow Wilson became the twenty-eighth president of the United States. The economic context had changed significantly. The U.S. economy and its industry, in particular, had been expanding for several years; in 1905, U.S. exports of manufactures exceeded those of foodstuffs for the first time (Kaufman, 1971). For U.S. producers it became increasingly evident that Europe would not purchase the surplus of manufactured goods they were producing. Interest in other markets grew noticeably and the promotion of foreign trade, especially in Latin America, became a central objective of the Wilson Administration. The "New Freedom" program embodied that vision. The Underwood-Simmons Act of October 1913, apart from imposing a federal income tax, significantly lowered import tax rates. The reasoning was that for U.S. exports to grow, foreigners had also to be able to sell to the United States (Kaufman, 1971).

An event that turned to be very relevant for the banking issues discussed during the 1890 Pan-American Conference was the creation of the Federal Reserve System in December 1913. In 1836 the charter of the Second Bank of the United States expired and it was not renewed due to concerns about its increasing power over economic life in the country (a fear whose echoes reverberated in the 1898 defeat of the International American Bank). After 1836, the U.S. banking system operated in a largely decentralized way, with many state-chartered banks and no federal regulation. There were violent fluctuations in the money supply and the economy and banking system remained very vulnerable to financial crises. Also, U.S. banks operated in local markets, with little or no participation in international trade and financial activities –the problem that the International American Bank of 1890 was supposed to solve.

In 1907 a more severe case of those recurrent financial crises convinced U.S. policy makers and voters that their banking structure needed major reforms. After several years of study and hearings in Congress, a proposal was presented that avoided banking concentration through the setting up of a decentralized system of regional reserve banks. At the same time, in order to provide some unity to the system, a central board would be established in Washington D.C. to control and coordinate the regional banks. The Federal Reserve Act, sponsored by Representative Carter Glass and Senator Robert L. Owen, was signed into law by President Wilson in December 1913.

The Federal Reserve Act allowed national banks to finance foreign trade, to open and maintain accounts in foreign countries, to appoint correspondents and establish agencies abroad, and to establish foreign branches with the approval of the Federal Reserve. These legislative changes eliminated the main barriers that had prevented American banks from operating in foreign trade and finance (Kaufman, 1971). Therefore, the issue that concerned the participants of the First Pan-American Conference in 1889/90 had been finally resolved. Of course, the 1890 International American Bank would have also had participation of Latin American investors, which was no longer the case with the newly approved legislation. By the summer of 1914 the First National City Bank of New York had already applied to open a branch in Buenos Aires, with the encouragement of the Argentine authorities (Kaufman, 1971). By 1918 that bank had already set up a dozen branches in Latin America (Thorp, 1998).

In the face of these developments, the issue of trade financing became less pressing. The economic problem that was becoming more important for trade was the weakening of the system of stable exchanges rates linked to the gold standard, which eventually broke down with World War I. The nature of a financial institution that could address exchange rate issues was different from the one linked to trade and investment financing. Those new challenges opened a different phase in the discussion of regional financial institutions.

c) Exchange Rates and the First World War

The outbreak of World War I in early August 1914 seriously disrupted trade and financial operations with Europe and reinforced the interest of both the United States and Latin American countries in strengthening regional ties. President Wilson in his December 1914 State of the Union Address to Congress summed up the issue: he noted that war was interrupting production and trade in Europe, affecting countries there, but also the countries that traded with the Europeans and that now "eagerly look to us to supply their all but empty markets." Woodrow Wilson argued that "this is particularly true of our own neighbors, the States, great and small, of Central and South America" and pointed to the "duty and opportunity" for the United States generated by that fact. He concluded: "here are markets which we must supply, and we must find the means of action" (Wilson, 1914).

The interest of Woodrow Wilson and his advisors in Latin America went beyond economic issues. Early in his presidency in March 1913 he had announced the end of "dollar diplomacy" arguing the "we can have no sympathy with those who seek to seize the power of government to advance their own personal interests or ambition." Later that same year at Mobile, Alabama, he addressed the Latin American republics, stating that "the United States will never again seek one additional foot of territory by conquest," and emphasized the importance of friendship, understanding, human rights, and national integrity, against material interests, that sometimes separate nations (Osgood, 1953; p.104 and quotations there).

These themes were further developed in January 1916, when President Wilson addressed the Second Pan-American Scientific Congress, in Washington D.C. His presentation explained the main points of a treaty that would embody his Pan-American vision. Afterwards, Woodrow Wilson asked his Secretary of State Robert Lansing, and Edward ("Colonel") House, a personal adviser, to work with the Latin American republics and reach agreements on those topics. This regional initiative would later become the basis for the 1920 League of Nations. As in other instances discussed here, the diplomatic dialogue started in the context of the Americas and then was expanded globally.

Regarding economic issues, the U.S. government also took other initiatives to deal with the financial and commercial disruptions of World War I. The U.S. Secretary of the Treasury, William Mc Adoo, working closely with the Secretary of Commerce, William Redfield, called for a Pan-American Financial Conference in 1915, which took place in Washington D.C. on May 24-29. With wartime disruptions in trade markets and financial losses due to several loans recalled by European banks, the Latin American republics quickly agreed.

The conference was called with the objective of establishing "closer and more satisfactory financial relations." The delegates raised again the issue of inter-American banking facilities; discussed the need that "U.S. banks and businessmen" provide "ample credit to Latin America;" and suggested the "prompt provision of the necessary organization and facilities for that purpose" (Comas, 2000; p.6). Regarding other financial issues McAdoo unsuccessfully pushed the idea of the expansion of the Federal Reserve banks, which would establish joint agencies in all the Latin American countries. This expansion would help banking businesses in the region, and would also "render a great service to American businessmen and bankers by furnishing credit reports and general information about trade and finance in the various countries in which they operate" (Proceedings of the First Pan-American Financial Conference, 1915, p.11).

A significant outcome of the conference was the creation of the International High Commission (note the title, even though it was regional in its membership). It had nine members appointed by the governments of the United States and Latin American countries. Its task was to unify commercial laws and to make recommendations on general trade and financial issues. This body, with different names, functioned until 1933, and helped to maintain continuity in the regional dialogue on financial, monetary, and banking issues.

After the Commission's first gathering in Buenos Aires in 1916 a three-member Central Executive Committee was created. It was chaired by McAdoo. This committee would coordinate subsequent meetings and implement the recommendations agreed in them. Another result was an ambitious program for trade development encompassing measures to ensure the uniformity of trade regulations, to expand transportation, communication, and banking, to promote the use of dollars in commercial transactions, and to stabilize exchange rates for the countries involved.

Regarding the crucial issue of exchange rates, there was a discussion to establish a gold-clearance fund with two main objectives: first, to avoid the physical movement of gold among countries to settle trade and financial claims; and, second, to determine clear, manageable and stable conversion rates across currencies. Threats to the international transportation of gold posed by WWI hostilities and the need to support trade led to a proposal that suggested the adoption of an international unit of account for the exchange rates. This idea was incorporated into a draft treaty. The system proposed would mirror the debt settlement mechanism existing among the twelve Federal Reserve banks and would thus function as an international trust fund, defined by clear property rights and procedures to settle transactions. The initiative was signed by ten Latin American republics and the United States, but further implementation was delayed by the war. The idea remained under study by the United States section of the International High Commission.

Another conference was scheduled to take place in 1917, but the meeting was postponed because the United States entered the global conflict that year. After the end of World War I, the Second Pan-

American Financial Conference met in Washington in 1920 and continued working on the 1916 Buenos Aires program. Communications, transportation, and uniform laws in trade matters took center stage again. There was a suggestion to create an Inter-American Tribunal for commercial and financial conflicts, as well as initiatives to avoid the double taxation of corporations. The establishment of branches of Latin American banks in the United States was also discussed (as noted before, the reverse was already happening, after the change in international banking legislation related to the creation of the Federal Reserve in 1913). The International High Commission created in 1915 was renamed, more adequately considering its regional coverage, as the Inter-American High Commission (IAHC) and functioned until 1933.[16]

An important financial issue discussed during the 1920 Conference was the proposal for a gold fund that had been analyzed during the 1916 meeting in Buenos Aires: one of the resolutions urged the Commission to continue working towards the adoption of the Gold Clearance Fund Convention (Bassett Moore, 1920). The Bankers Magazine (1920) added, anticipating things to come, that although this plan covered the hemisphere, "it contains a principle...which has lately attracted wide attention and which may prove to be of incalculable value to the world in the future" (p.194). In fact, although not implemented at that time, the proposal to establish an international gold fund to stabilize exchange rates and trade passed by the Second Financial Congress of American Republics constituted an antecedent for the creation of the International Monetary Fund a quarter century later.

The end of the Wilson Administration prevented these measures from being implemented. The Harding Administration took a more unilateral approach to hemispheric issues (Kaufman, 1971) and did not hold regional conferences. The Inter-American High Commission, however, continued to meet, which may have reduced the need for convening more formal gatherings.

The importance of an international gold fund declined considering that the hostilities had ended and exchange rates stabilized with the return of many countries to the gold standard. Therefore, the

---

[16] As discussed below, the IAHC reassumed functions in 1939 with the new name of the Inter-American Financial and Economic Advisory Commission (IAFEAC). This was the body that drafted the Charter for the 1940 Inter-American Bank). In 1945 the IAFEAC became the Inter-American Economic and Social Council, which was later incorporated as part of the Organization of American States.

proposal for a Gold Clearance Fund Convention dragged along for some time. In 1922, the Treasury and the State Departments, which were considering the same approach on a wider scale, took over the issue for further study and the idea of a separate regional arrangement was eventually abandoned.

During the 1920s there were two other general Pan-American Conferences: the fifth in Santiago (March-May 1923) and the sixth in La Habana (January-February, 1928). The issue of a regional bank did not resurface (Comas, 2000). The Santiago Conference was considered by Inman "the most far-reaching in its discussions and actions…since the one at Panama in 1826" (p. 91). It focused, however, mostly on political issues (such as the formation of an American League of Nations, which the Harding Administration opposed after the failure of approving the League of Nations by the U.S. Congress) and on issues of disarmament.[17] During the La Habana Conference, participating countries confronted with mounting strains in the world gold standard system that had been reestablished after World War I, suggested the study of a common currency and measures to counteract growing volatility in exchange rates (Comas, 2000).

d) The Credit Binge of the 1920s

The early twentieth century witnessed a substantial shift in the global balance of power, with important implications for international trade and financial matters. Regarding trade, the United States, by 1913, was already ahead of the United Kingdom as the main exporter to Mexico, Central American, the Spanish-speaking Caribbean countries, Venezuela, Colombia, Ecuador, and, marginally, Peru (Smith, 1996, Table A1, p.337). World War I and its aftermath, which weakened all European competitors, coupled with the new Panama Canal that opened in 1914, further consolidated the position of the United States as the main trade partner for most Latin American countries.

In financial terms, by the end of 1919 the United States had become a net international creditor by over 3.3 billion dollars (about 40 billion dollars in March 2010 money), whereas before World War I it had been a net debtor for about the same amount (Thorp, 1998). At the same time, U.S. financial links with Latin America deepened after

---

[17] Among other things it also decided to include the issue of women rights in subsequent conferences to analyze the means to abolish the inequalities with men regarding civil and political rights (Comas, 2000).

the war. U.S. private foreign investment, which, as a whole, rose from 3.5 billion dollars in 1914 to 6.4 billion dollars in 1919, increased rapidly in Mexican mining, oil, and railways, Peruvian copper, Chilean nitrates, Colombian bananas, and in many Central American countries (Thorp, 1998). Also, U.S. banks expanded fast in the region: by 1926, there were sixty-one branches of U.S. banks in Latin America (Thorp, 1998). This expansion of international financial facilities in the Americas had been the objective of the International American Bank, but now the capital of those institutions came only from United States instead of the mix of private investors from North, Central, and South American countries envisaged in 1890.

Substantial needs for capital in Latin American countries coexisted with an increasingly evident trade asymmetry with the United States, then supplying most of the imports in the region but buying fewer of its exports. As a continental economy, with a large domestic market and abundant natural resources, the United States depended less on trade than the United Kingdom and continued with its traditional protectionist policies. The combination of greatly expanded financing from the United States to Latin America in the 1920s (the result of aggressive U.S. bankers and eager Latin borrowers that quickly became over-indebted) and of U.S. trade restrictions that limited the exports needed to pay for those loans was creating serious external imbalances for the region.[18] Also, many loans were largely unmonitored and in several cases were not accompanied by productive investments that would help pay for the debt that was being generated. The seeds for the subsequent financial crisis were planted (Thorp, 1998).

There were also serious trade and financial imbalances at the global level. The United States and France were accumulating gold reserves through trade surpluses, while the United Kingdom, which had come back to the gold standard at the pre-war overvalued

---

[18] Within the United States, internationally-oriented banking interests frequently collided with the economic nationalism of policy makers throughout the 1920s, and, usually, trade protectionists had the upper hand. Thus, although the United States had become a major lender, U.S. authorities had reversed the wartime commitments to low and flexible tariffs, making more difficult for foreign borrowers to service their loans through expanded exports to the U.S. market (Frieden, 1988). During the debt crisis of the 1980s that affected LAC countries a similar discrepancy between trade and finance interests also emerged, but with a different configuration: U.S. exporters to LAC countries complained that the harsh repayment conditions to the U.S. creditor banks were strangling demand for imported products in the region.

exchange rate, suffered from trade deficits and weak economic performance. The gold standard was operating at non-equilibrium exchange-rate parities, particularly between the United States and the United Kingdom, and without an anchor country committed to make the system work (Eichengreen, 1996). The fractures in the international economic system were deepening. When the Federal Reserve tightened monetary policies in 1929, concerned about an overheating U.S. economy, the Great Depression started. The subsequent crash of the U.S. stock market, although not necessarily the most important trigger of the economic crisis that followed, became its most visible manifestation.

Third Phase

The Great Depression, World War II, and the Inter-American Bank.

a) The Great Depression and Early Regional Responses

With the onset of the Great Depression in the early 1930s, the capital flows that had flooded Latin America during the 1920s dried up. Also, as a result of global deflationary forces linked to a badly managed gold standard in the United States and Europe, the prices of primary commodities that were Latin America's main exports collapsed even before 1929: Argentine wheat peaked in mid 1927 and experienced a sharp decline afterwards; Cuban sugar began to drop after it peaked in early 1928; and Brazilian coffee, since early 1929 (Thorp, 1998). The unit value of the main Latin American exports fell by more than 50 percent between 1928 and 1932, with mineral exporters (Chile, Bolivia, and Mexico) and Cuba as the most affected countries (Thorp, 1992 and 1998).

Protectionism increased in the United States with the passage of the Smoot-Hawley Tariff Act of 1930. Similarly, the United Kingdom approved the British Abnormal Importations Act in 1931 and the British Commonwealth Preferences were adopted during the Ottawa meeting in 1932. Other countries such as France, Germany, and Japan also increased protectionist measures and implemented discriminatory trade arrangements for regions and countries under their political control or influence (Thorp, 1998).

With the United States and European countries focused on their markets and areas of influence, export volumes also fell precipitously in Latin America and the impact of the economic depression in the region turned severe. The real burden of the external debt became magnified by declining prices and falling lending flows, thus preventing even those countries with the best credit ratings in Latin America from obtaining new loans during the Great Depression. Several Latin American countries defaulted on their international debts.

Against this backdrop, the Pan-American Agricultural Conference of 1930 contemplated the creation of an Inter-American Agricultural Bank with branches in the region, which would extend rural credits, finance regional exporters during economic downturns and facilitate the expansion of trade. In the end, the delegates decided to drop the idea, fearing that such financial institution "would seem to hold the possibility of the subjugation of South American agriculture by Wall Street" (Washington Post, September 24, 1930).

After that, economic issues were again taken up by the Fourth Pan-American Commercial Conference that met in Washington (October 1931). There was a proposal to establish a Pan-American Economic Agency, but the conference ended without specific resolutions. Discussions were postponed until the Seventh International Conference of American States, which was going to take place in Montevideo, in December 1933. The election of Franklin Delano Roosevelt in November of 1932 as the new president of the United States changed significantly the U.S. political landscape, with implications on many fronts, including the relations between Latin America and the United States.

b) The Roosevelt Administration, the "Good Neighbor" Policy, and the Evolution of Regional Financial Issues

Early in 1933, President Roosevelt unveiled a new approach to hemispheric relations: the "Good Neighbor" policy. As good neighbor, the United States would respect "obligations and the sanctity of agreements," promising respect and equality to the Latin American republics. FDR's inaugural address spelled out the contents of this new policy, stressing non intervention but also non interference in other countries' domestic issues. It implied abandoning the conceptual framework of Theodore Roosevelt's Corollary to the Monroe Doctrine. Also, the U.S. government promised to follow local laws rather than unilaterally enforcing the protection of U.S. property and citizens in foreign countries. The numerous and failed military interventions in countries like Nicaragua and Cuba had evidenced the limits of hard power in the region, and commercial interests, now less affected by European competition, were going to be better served by the new policy based on diplomacy, economic cooperation, and cordial relations. Finally, the advance of the Third Reich in Germany and the presence of Mussolini in Italy, suggested the possibility of another world war, which provided the incentives for the United States to concentrate on hemispheric affairs.[19]

By and large, the Roosevelt Administration in the early 1930s tried to maintain some distance from European engagements and gave substantial priority to Pan-American affairs. The Seventh Inter-American Conference, held in Montevideo in late 1933, was called amid a growing awareness of the financial havoc created by the Great Depression. Two resolutions (XXXVIII and V) emphasized the need for greater economic cooperation in the Americas. One of them proposed again the creation of a common currency in the Americas. Also, based on a proposal by Peru and Uruguay, the creation of an agency for economic and financial cooperation in the region was recommended. This institution would include a Board, a Consultative Economic Committee, and an inter-American Bank. This financial institution would have the functions of a continental Central Bank, helping to establish and promote regional credit and capital flows, and collaborating in the reconstruction of sound national monetary conditions. According to the conference's resolution, the institution would be controlled by the Central Banks of the region and it would be based in a Latin American city. Its main functions would be to regulate credit and monetary issues and to promote capital flows, operating in a framework complemented by other measures of financial liberalization discussed during the conference.

A subsequent meeting to decide the specific details of the bank did not take place and the subject was postponed for several years until the Eighth Inter-American Conference that took place in Lima in 1938 (Maisch, 2004).

The other resolution called for the participating countries to lower their tariffs through trade negotiations, setting a precedent for what would later be the General Agreement on Tariffs and Trade (GATT) (Maisch, 2004).[20]

---

[19] Helleiner (2006) also points to a change in perceptions and attitudes towards the region, triggered by the Great Depression. In his view, public hearings on the lending practices of American bankers in Latin America during the previous decade created a sense of solidarity based on the idea that the region had also fallen prey to the same group of financiers that was blamed for the economic problems in the United States.
[20] The Seventh Conference also introduced the issue of rights and protection of native communities and proposed the organization of a conference on those topics (Comas, 2000).

Within the Roosevelt Administration, the officials in charge of the international agenda, Secretary of State Cordell Hull, a staunch proponent of trade liberalization, and Secretary of the Treasury Henry Morgenthau, another internationalist, had different perspectives about how to approach the international economic agenda. Secretary of State Hull was an advocate of private-sector approaches and his main institutional remit was related to trade and diplomatic issues. In contrast, Morgenthau was more convinced of the need of government intervention and his Department covered the financial aspects of the international agenda. The bureaucratic and conceptual differences between both Secretaries would color how the Roosevelt Administration interacted with Latin America in economic affairs.

During 1934 there was a flurry of initiatives in the United States related to different economic issues. In January, the Exchange Stabilization Fund was established as part of the Gold Reserve Act with the purpose of stabilizing the exchange value of the U.S. dollar through selling and buying gold and foreign currencies. The Export-Import Bank was also created that year with the objective of extending loans to U.S. exporters. Finally, the U.S. Congress also approved the Reciprocal Trade Agreements Act. As in earlier episodes, the Americas would be a testing ground for financial and commercial policies that would later be extended to other regions.

Secretary Hull began to pursue bilateral treaties for trade liberalization, reversing the effects of the 1930 Smoot-Hawley Tariff Act. Falling commodity prices, weak export markets, and scarce credit, all worsened by the Smoot-Hawley Tariff Act and the Ottawa Conference, led several Latin countries to embrace the U.S. initiatives to expand trade through bilateral treaties. The United States signed trade agreements with Cuba and Honduras (1934), Guatemala (1935), Costa Rica and Colombia (1936) and El Salvador (1937). These countries were heavily dependent on the U.S. market for their export products. On the other hand, Argentina, Chile, Uruguay, and other countries mainly in South America were not so dependent, and they did not reach agreements with the United States. Thus, the negotiations repeated much of what had happened with the reciprocal trade approach of Secretary of State Blaine during the Harrison Administration in the early 1890s. Despite the somewhat limited nature of the treaties signed, Latin America welcomed the initiatives as a departure from Depression-era protectionism.

U.S. commercial focus on the region was also a response to Germany's efforts to establish a strong economic and political presence in Latin America. The European power was trying to buy raw materials, paying with a special currency which only allowed purchases of German imports.[21] A prominent scenario for this contest was Brazil, a country that, to the dismay of the Roosevelt Administration, had bilateral trade agreements with both the United States and Germany. More generally, the United States feared that Germany's commercial ascendancy in Latin America would lead to greater political presence from that country, and the establishment of a German sphere of influence, which, in a worst-case scenario, could potentially culminate with the takeover of the Panama Canal.

In 1936 the Roosevelt Administration decided to use the Exchange Stabilization Fund to provide a loan to Mexico to support its currency, amid concerns about the financial situation in that country and the potentially destabilizing effects of a debt and banking crisis there. This action anticipated several features of future IMF operations, including the fact that the loan was structured as an exchange of currencies instead of a direct loan (Bordo and Schwartz, 2001). [22]

The Inter-American Conference for the Maintenance of Peace, in Buenos Aires (January 1936), took place within a framework of increasing global hostility and U.S. concerns about the influence of Nazism in the Americas. The situation in Spain, where Francisco Franco had been proclaimed head of the rebels against the Republic in October 1936, was also considered by the Roosevelt Administration as increasing the possibility of fascist influence in Latin America. Therefore, the primary purpose of the Buenos Aires conference was the discussion of regional security issues. President Roosevelt's participation in the conference evidenced how important the security situation in the region was becoming for the United States.

---

[21] Germany's investment in the region appears to have been also important at the time, but precise data is more difficult to assess due to the prevalence of local agents that acted as screens for the true owners, among other factors (see Escudé and Cisneros, 2000).

[22] Currently, when a country borrows from the IMF, the operation is considered a swap of currencies: the debtor country gives its own currency to the IMF in exchange for dollars or other reserve currencies, and pays interests on the latter. The repayment of the loan is presented as a "buyback" of the borrowing country's currency.

It was agreed that in the case of war the American countries would consult and cooperate to maintain peace in the continent. In the area of economic and financial affairs there were two resolutions. One called for a financial conference to study monetary stabilization issues and the possible lifting of exchange controls among the countries of the Americas.[23] The other resolution recommended the inclusion in the following conference, which was going to take place in Lima in 1938, of a proposal for the creation of a regional economic and financial institution, along the lines of the ideas that had been presented in the Montevideo Conference of 1933.

In general, the U.S. position expressed by the State Department up to the time of the outbreak of World War II in 1939 was that Latin America had enough financial support as a result of the operations of U.S. private banks and the Export-Import Bank. The U.S. Treasury, on the other hand, was leaning towards a more direct approach: as early as October 1938, Harry Dexter White, a high official in that Department, had drafted, under instructions and direct guidance from Secretary Morgenthau, a Treasury document to President Roosevelt outlining a large-scale public program of economic aid for Latin America and China. Roosevelt was advised to "use our great financial strength to help safeguard future peace for United States and to make your 'Good Neighbor' policy really effective" (quoted in Green, 1971, p.46).

With international tension increasing, the Eighth Inter-American Conference met in Lima on December 9-27, 1938. The delegates reiterated their commitment to maintaining peace, democracy, and individual liberties in the region, while respecting the sovereignty of the participating countries. In economic terms, there were again proposals to reduce tariff and non-tariff barriers to trade (Resolution II) and renewed calls to increase economic and commercial cooperation and consultation within the hemisphere. In particular, the Colombian delegation presented a draft "Treaty on Inter-American Trade Liberalization and Economic Non-Aggression" to institutionalize a system of free trade, but the idea was not approved (Maisch, 2004).

The conference requested the Pan-American Union to continue its work on economic and financial matters, and established a commission of experts to study the convenience of creating an Inter-American Economic and Financial Institute. It also decided to organize

---

[23] Those controls had been imposed as a result of the disruptions in financial and trade flows associated with the Great Depression.

meetings of the Financial Ministers at least annually, and the first meeting was set for Guatemala in 1939 (Comas, 2000; Maisch, 2004).

By that time, and despite Germany's growing commercial presence before the British blockade, the United States had become the leading trade partner for every major country in the region. The only exception was Argentina, which continued to trade mainly with the United Kingdom (Smith, 1996, Table A2, p. 338). [24]

In terms of economic assistance, U.S. policies, at least as pursued by the State Department until 1939, continued to use the treatment of U.S. private economic interests by Latin American governments as a main criterion to evaluate whether or not to support those countries. Expropriation of U.S. oil companies by the Bolivian and Mexican governments triggered various forms of economic pressure, involving the withholding of loans and technical assistance from the Export-Import Bank and others as well as attempts to block cooperation from other countries.

The U.S. Treasury under Morgenthau, and contrary to the pattern that would prevail later, had a more positive view regarding the involvement of governments in financial and economic matters and it was more willing to provide financial support to countries that were considered to be under the pressure of the Axis. Therefore, in March 1939, and expanding on the document of October 1938, White drafted another long Treasury document outlining a massive foreign aid program for the Latin American countries, and also China and Russia, all countries and regions deemed to be at risk of succumbing to the pressure of the Axis powers (Green, 1971 and Rees, 1973).

The outbreak of World War II in early September 1939, with the German invasion of Poland and subsequent declarations of war on Germany by the United Kingdom, France, and other countries, provided a new context for the debate about international economic and financial matters within the Roosevelt Administration.

---

[24] The triangle of separate interests among the United States, the United Kingdom and Argentina was a permanent cause of friction. Argentina enjoyed a separate source of income through its exports to the United Kingdom, which facilitated the Southern republic's efforts to resist U.S. attempts at regional hegemony. And there were also frictions between the United States and the United Kingdom: the latter did not want to be displaced from its main market in South America, and the United States disliked both U.K. economic presence in the region and the fact that it provided the economic resources for the regional rebel (see, for instance, Kirby, 1981).

c) The Inter-American Bank

Following the start of hostilities in Europe, the American republics met later in September 1939 for the First Meeting of Consultation of Foreign Ministers of the Americas (Panama, September-October 1939). Obviously, security issues received the greatest attention; but there were also recommendations that the participating countries make joint efforts to protect their economic and financial institutions, maintain fiscal equilibrium, develop trade, expand their industries, ensure the stability of their currencies and increase their agricultural production (Inman, 1965; Comas, 2000).

During the meeting, Latin American countries asked again for the creation of a new financial institution, which, in their view, should apply a multilateral approach instead of the bilateralism that they considered was characteristic of the Export-Import Bank. Within this framework, some of the topics that were discussed regarding the potential new bank included government guarantees of private loans, U.S. veto power in a regional institution, and the need to benefit from commercial access to the U.S. market in order for the Latin American countries to be able to pay their financial debts.

The United States tried to deflect the pressure for the creation of a regional financial institution by authorizing the Export-Import Bank to also provide loans to governments, as many Latin countries had asked. In the meeting Sumner Welles, then the State Department official responsible for Latin American affairs, argued that financial resources should be assigned along "sound and non competitive lines," using the private banking system and the Export-Import Bank. U.S. bankers coincided with the State Department about the emphasis on the private sector; the Export-Import Bank (which, after the initial doubts, U.S. financiers realized that it was supporting, and not displacing, their own operations) was as far as they would go regarding acceptance of public sector's involvement in finances (Green, 1971).

On the other hand, Latin Americans wanted a multilateral approach that transcended both the private sector, which they saw too short-term oriented, and the Export-Import Bank, whose decisions they considered unpredictable due to constantly changing political considerations. With the leadership of the Mexican delegation, a draft for the creation of a permanent inter-American financial institution was presented during the meeting.

The U.S. government was not ready to move in that direction and therefore the meeting only adopted a resolution creating the Inter-American Financial and Economic Advisory Committee (IAFEAC) with twenty-one representatives, one from every American state (Comas, 2000). However, and because of the insistence of the Latin American delegations, the committee included among its tasks the study of the need, form and conditions for the establishment of an inter-American banking institution that would ensure cooperation between Treasuries and Central Banks in the region. It was also agreed that Financial Ministers meet as needed to discuss those economic matters.

As Green (1971) notes, the Panama Conference may have been a turning point in the U.S. thinking about the issue of a regional bank: the Roosevelt Administration noticed the strong support among Latin American countries for that idea and, therefore, decided to work on a draft of its own within the framework of the IAFEAC.

The start of World War II marked a shift towards the U.S. Treasury approach that had been advocated by Harry Dexter White, with encouragement and guidance from Secretary Morgenthau. Hemispheric security was going to be emphasized over the protection of private economic interests. The expansion of economic assistance as part of the "Good Neighbor" policy was based on concerns about the possibility that the region could come under extra-hemispheric influences if the United States ignored the problems that Latin America was facing.

As European markets closed, in 1939 the State Department presented some proposals on trade issues (its side of the international economic portfolio), floating a plan for a governmental trade arrangement that would commercialize Latin American exports in a centralized fashion. Finally, the scheme was abandoned. The reasons were both doubts from Latin American countries, which feared U.S. control over the scheme, and U.S. concerns about possible repercussions in Asia, where Japan could demand a similar scheme to consolidate its presence in East Asia (Green, 1971).

Almost immediately after the Panama meeting, and following the resolution in Lima the year before, the First Meeting of Finance Ministers of the American Republics took place in Guatemala (November, 1939). Again, the idea of a common "monetary system" in the Americas was proposed. It was also agreed to ask the recently created IAFEAC the urgent study of the convenience and possibility of the creation of an institution with functions of monetary compensation and investment, for which the Mexican delegation presented again a draft proposal (see Villaseñor, 1941 and 1948; Comas, 2000).

The IAFEAC began its work in Washington on November 15, 1939 with delegates from the twenty-one American countries, assisted by a group of experts from the U.S. Departments of State and Treasury, the Board of Governors of the Federal Reserve System, and the Federal Loan Agency.[25] The work of the committee was divided into several subcommittees. The one in charge of monetary and financial issues was chaired by Sumner Welles from the U.S. State Department and included delegates from Argentina, Bolivia, Colombia, Ecuador, Mexico, and Peru. This sub-committee prepared a draft, based on a memorandum prepared by the delegates of the United States and Mexico, which was forwarded to the full committee on November 28 (Comas, 2000). But before the proposal was presented, it had been studied in detail by the U.S. Treasury, where Harry Dexter White had a direct involvement in the drafting of the charter of the new institution.

On February 7, 1940, the committee adopted a resolution recommending to the governments of the American republics the establishment of the Inter-American Bank, and submitted drafts for a treaty, charter, and by-laws. Different governments presented comments and suggestions, which led to some adjustments, and a new version was later presented (Broide, 1961; Comas, 2000). On April 16, 1940, the IAFEAC approved the final text.

d) *Structure and Operations of the Inter-American Bank (I-AB)* [26]

The proposal envisaged a capital of 100 million dollars (about 1,500 million dollars in March 2010 currency) for the Inter-American Bank, consisting of 1,000 shares with a par value of 100,000 dollars each, to be paid for in gold or in U.S. dollars. Each country would subscribe

---

[25] In fact, the large presence of U.S. officials participating in the deliberations and in the drafting of documents generated uneasiness among some LAC delegates, who felt outnumbered and, at times, marginalized in the negotiations.

[26] This section is mostly based on the Federal Reserve Bulletin of June 1940, where the proposed legislation was published. The references and quotes come from that publication, except otherwise noted.

twenty basic shares plus an additional amount of shares according to their wealth and size.[27]

The objectives of the bank, as enumerated in the Charter, were very ambitious: (1) to facilitate prudent investment of funds; (2) to "assist in stabilizing the currencies of American Republics; encourage general direct exchanges of the currencies of American Republics; encourage the maintenance of adequate monetary reserves; promote the use and distribution of gold and silver; and facilitate monetary equilibrium"; (3) to function as a clearing house to facilitate the transfer of international payments; (4) to increase international trade in the Americas; (5) to promote the development of industry, public utilities, mining, agriculture, commerce, and finance; (6) to foster economic cooperation in general; (7) to conduct research in technology of agriculture, industry, public utilities, mining, and commerce; (8) to do research and provide expert advice on public finance, exchange, banking, and money; and (9) to promote publication of data and information.

The operational powers were also vast. According to the Charter, the Inter-American Bank was authorized to: (1) approve short-term, intermediate, and long-term loans and credits in any currency and in precious metals to participating governments and to fiscal agencies, central banks, political subdivisions, and individuals; (2) buy, sell, hold and deal in the obligations and securities; (3) guarantee in whole or in part credits and loans; (4) act as a clearing house of funds, balances, checks, drafts, and acceptances; (5) buy, sell, hold, and deal in precious metals, currencies, and foreign exchange for its own account and for the account of others; (6) issue or sell debentures and other securities and obligations of the bank; (7) accept deposits (paying interests only to governments); (8) discount and rediscount bills, acceptances, and other obligations and instruments of credit; (9)

---

[27] Given that the notion of Gross Domestic Product had not been yet developed, the level of exports was used as the indicator to define the amount of additional shares to be subscribed by each country. The countries were divided in groups as follows: Group A: Costa Rica, Ecuador, El Salvador, Haiti, Honduras, Nicaragua and Paraguay (each country would subscribe five shares); Group B: Dominican Republic, Guatemala and Panama (ten shares each country); Group C: Bolivia (fifteen shares); Group D: Uruguay (twenty shares); Group E: Peru (twenty-five shares); Group F: Chile, Colombia and Cuba (thirty shares each country); Group G; Mexico and Venezuela (thirty-five shares each country); Group H: Argentina, Brazil and United States (fifty shares each country).

rediscount bills, acceptances, and instruments of credit taken from the bank's portfolio; (10) open and maintain deposits and arrange with governments and banking institutions to act as agent or correspondent for the bank; (11) act as agent or correspondent of other entities; (12) prepare financial and economic studies and publish reports; (13) buy, sell, and deal in cable transfers, accept bills and drafts drawn upon the bank, and issue letters of credit; (14) acquire, own, hold, use or dispose of such real and personal property as may be necessary; and (15) "exercise incidental powers necessary and proper to carry out the powers expressly authorized in the Charter."

From that extensive list, it was noted at the time that one of the main functions envisioned for the bank was accepting deposits from central banks and operating as an "inter-American clearing house," with the power to "discount commercial paper covering goods moving between countries in the Western Hemisphere" (The Washington Post, November 24, 1939).

The voting power was based on twenty votes for each country based on the minimum shares and one vote for each additional share subscribed. Therefore, the United States did not have a majority voting power and it also seemed to fall short of veto power for the important decisions that required a four-fifths majority vote.[28]

The directors of the Inter-American Bank were appointed by the governments representing the countries as shareholders and they were responsible to those governments alone. The president of the bank was elected from the Board for two years renewable. The institution was established for a period of twenty years, which could be extended.

All operations of the bank in a specific country needed the non-objection from the respective government and, in the case of loans of more than two years to the private sector, government guarantees were also required. Before approving a medium or long-term loan, the bank would commission a report prepared by an externally appointed committee of experts.

---

[28] The United States would have had 70 (50 plus the 20 basic shares, or a mere 7 percent of the shares) and could block decisions requiring super majorities only forging alliances with other countries to achieve the 201 votes needed (i.e. the more than the 20 percent of the voting power that would deny the formation of a four-fifths majority). In the financial institutions that were later created the United States had a greater percentage of shares, which facilitated the formation of coalitions to exercise a potential veto power, and, on some key decisions, it could block a vote alone.

An important innovation highlighted by U.S. high officials during the Congressional hearings was that borrowing countries would be able to repay loans in local currency (even though the original loan was in dollars). Those repayments would then work as a rotating fund in that country for loans to other projects (a feature later replicated in the Fund for Special Operations of the Inter-American Development Bank), until the balance of payment conditions improved enough to pay back the dollar loan (Broide, 1961). The U.S. dollar was defined as the base currency to determine the values of the Latin American currencies.

The convention for the establishment of the Inter-American Bank was signed by Under-Secretary of State Sumner Welles along with representatives of Colombia, the Dominican Republic, Ecuador, Mexico, Nicaragua, Paraguay, and Bolivia, at the Pan-American Union in Washington, on May 10, 1940. Brazil signed on May 13. The U.S. Executive sent the treaty to Congress. In its submission to the U.S. Senate, President Franklin Roosevelt argued that "the establishment of an Inter-American Bank would be a step of major importance in the development of inter-American financial and economic cooperation and the economic implementation of good-neighbor policy" (U.S. Senate, 1941).

During the hearings at the Committee of Foreign Affairs of the Senate (May 5 and 6, 1941) several high officials presented testimonies defending the creation of the Inter-American Bank, including Assistant Secretary of State A.A. Berle, Emilio Collado (at that time with the U.S. State Department), and members of the Federal Reserve, the Federal Loan Administration, and others.[29]

Berle argued that "in the past, movements of capital have been regarded by Latin Americans as, frankly, imperialist. The proposed bank would facilitate capital movements which are worked out not merely…to make a profit, but following the more careful plans of the various governments involved with a steady view of development of the country." He also noted that Latin American citizens took their savings out of the region and sent their money to "New York or other monetary markets" mostly because of concerns about their own currencies and instability of exchange rates; now the Inter-American Bank, by preserving the value of the savings, would allow the use of

---

[29] The following quotes are from "Hearings before a Subcommittee of the Committee on Foreign Relations United State Senate: A Convention for the Establishment of an Inter-American Bank, signed on behalf of the, United States of America on May, 1940" U.S. Senate, May 5 and 6, 1941. United States Government Printing Office, Washington, 1941. See also Broide (1961), and Comas (2000).

those funds for the development of the region. At the same time, this retention of savings in the region would alleviate the pressure on the United States to provide funds for the development of Latin American countries. Berle also warned that there would be a time when imbalances in the credit position of the countries in the region hemispheres would prevent the collection of loans in dollars, but that, in those cases, the innovation of the revolving fund in local currency would facilitate the eventual collection of the loans.

One of the sources of financing for the Inter-American Bank was the issuing of its own debt in international markets to fund projects in Latin American countries, presumably under the collective guarantee of the signatory countries.[30] In this regard, Berle argued that U.S. investors who bought debt instruments issued by the Inter-American Bank would benefit because of the greater certainty of repayment. The reason was that the more careful analysis and supervision of the projects financed by the bank would lead to operations that strengthened the national economies where the money was used, which Berle contrasted with the failures of the past when investors lost money in unsupervised investments in foreign countries.

But a main selling point was geopolitical: Berle told the Senate Committee that "we have at least conceived the possibility that military events may move badly in Europe," and that then the Axis powers could "use their buying power politically to establish governments…they approve" In that event, the Inter-American Bank would allow the United States "to step in so that no country shall be coerced" (U.S. Senate, 1941).

Responding to criticisms about overlapping functions with other financial institutions, Administration officials also suggested during the hearing that many operations of the Export-Import Bank would be transferred to the Inter-American Bank once it was created.

e) The "Super Bank" that Wasn't

As it was conceived, the Inter-American Bank was a powerful institution that combined the functions of a) an investment bank; b) an

---

[30] This mechanism anticipated what would become the main form of funding for the future international banks, such as the World Bank and the IDB. That guarantee, particularly the one granted by the United States, would allow the institutions to borrow in world markets, leveraging the far smaller portion of paid-in capital that taxpayers, form all member countries, invested in cash in those institutions.

international stabilization fund with some Central Bank powers; c) an ordinary commercial bank, and d) a center of technical and economic research to promote economic development. In general, the structure of this institution anticipated many of the features that were later present in the World Bank and the International Monetary Fund, created as a result of the 1944 Bretton Woods conference.

The sheer ambition of the bank project proved intimidating: newspapers called it a "giant Federal Reserve system" and "super-bank," while in Congress, some legislators urged their peers not to "panic into granting a charter...to a Mexican-inspired institution designed to serve domestic and foreign politics" (The Washington Post, November 24, 1939).[31]

The debates in Congress repeated some old arguments but also anticipated themes that would reemerge about two decades later in relation with the creation of the Inter-American Development Bank. For instance, doubts were expressed about the fact that the Latin American countries had a majority in the decision-making process. Also, some critics worried that, once the bank was approved, the Inter-American Bank would become a twenty-year commitment from the United States, with little control over the institution during that period.

Concerns in the United States about the expanding influence of the government in the economy under the Roosevelt Administration also affected the debate about the Inter-American Bank, which was considered by its critics as a significant public interference in the private sphere. A more limited discussion, but important for the approval of the legislation needed to create the new institution, took place between an Executive branch, which was becoming increasingly more powerful, and a Congress concerned about losing its constitutional role and authority. Also, echoing later debates about the impact of development aid, Robert Taft, a powerful Republican Senator and presidential candidate, doubted that loans for developing countries like Brazil (the Export-Import Bank had then approved a loan for the Volta Redonda steel mill) would really benefit the United States (Green, p. 68).

Yet, probably the most effective opposition came from the U.S. banks that feared the competition of a new and powerful financial institution. In May 1940, the authorities of the National City Bank of New York, the largest U.S. bank with operations in South America,

---

[31] This refers to the role played by the Mexican delegation during the discussions of the bank scheme (see Villaseñor 1941 and 1948; Comas, 2000).

sent a communication to the U.S. Secretary of the Treasury complaining. They argued that the Inter-American Bank could open branches "across the street" from each one of the offices of the National City Bank in South America, and "damage the business of this and other commercial banks" due to the privileged position regarding taxation, exchange controls, and other advantages as a governmental institution (Green, 1971, p. 68).

The officials of the U.S. Treasury and State Departments in charge of the project tried to assuage those fears by offering an amendment to the internal by-laws of the Inter-American Bank that would forbid the institution from entering into the shorter-term operations that were of greatest interest for the private banks. But being an amendment to the internal by-laws of the bank and not a modification of the Charter, this proposal implied a weaker remedy than what the private banks wanted. Also, Berle's comments at the hearings of the Foreign Affairs Committee had not been terribly reassuring for private sector banks: first, he criticized private sector finance operations based only on the "profit motive;" and then, he suggested that Latin America's savings, a percentage of which was deposited in New York, would now be partially absorbed by the Inter-American Bank and stay in the region.

The bankers found an ally in legendary Senator Carter Glass, by then eighty two years old. He had been a former Chairman of the influential Senate Banking and Currency Committee and was at that time the Chairman of the powerful Appropriations Committee (in 1941 he also became President Pro-Tempore of the Senate, position he held until his death in 1946).

Senator Glass, as co-sponsor of the bill that created the Federal Reserve in 1913 and also the 1933 Glass-Steagall Act that separated commercial and investment operations of banks, had always been wary of concentration of banking power. Therefore, he became concerned about the vast powers of the new institution, which appeared to undo all the checks and balances he had helped put in place both with the Federal Reserve and the Glass-Steagall Acts. Senator Glass was able to convince his colleagues that his committee also had to hold hearings on this important topic. Once this was granted, he basically killed the legislation by not taking action on it.[32] The Roosevelt Administration made several

---

[32] It did not help the treatment of the proposed legislation that Senator Glass was already in bad health, attending Senate sessions sporadically and that he basically

attempts to revive the process and/or work around Glass's committee, but it did not succeed. Among Latin American countries, only Mexico, whose delegation had played an important role in the conceptualization of the bank, obtained a rapid ratification from its Congress.[33]

Notwithstanding all the problems in the U.S. Congress, hopes about the materialization of the institution had not disappeared. Therefore, in the Third Conference of Ministers of Foreign Relations in Rio de Janeiro (January, 1942) there was a recommendation encouraging those countries that had not yet ratified the Convention creating the Inter-American Bank to study the proposal and inform the IAFEAC as soon as possible about their decision (Comas, 2000). Of course, the main issue of the conference was the definite involvement of the United States in World War II after the Japanese attack to Pearl Harbor on December 7, 1941. The conference recommended that the Latin American republics break diplomatic relations with Japan, Germany, and Italy.

f) The Inter-American Bank and the Creation of the Bretton Woods Institutions

With the United States now completely immersed in World War II, the Inter-American Bank and related economic initiatives moved to the backburner. The immediate concerns for the United States in the Americas turned to the provision of raw materials for the war effort, and the strengthening of security ties within the region. At the same time, the United States began to move to a global vision of the problems it had to face once the world conflict was over (Green, 1971).

---

stopped going to the Senate after 1942 –an absence that continued for the next four years until his death in 1946.

[33] Eduardo Villaseñor, the head of the Mexican delegation to the meeting in Guatemala in 1939, presented the case for the Bank in an article in Foreign Affairs in 1941. He argued the importance of investment loans for economic development such as "land improvements" designed to increase yields; "the modernization of factories"; hydroelectric plants; hotels, "steamship lines and air routes," and the like. On the other hand, Villaseñor argued that it was not appropriate for the Bank to offer loans for general support of the budget or the balance of payments –an argument that anticipated debates that took place several decades later at the multilateral development banks during the 1980s debt crisis. Even after the proposed legislation was retired from the U.S. Congress, Villaseñor continued to write in support of the creation of a regional bank, noting in 1948 that a "permanent, organic and definitive solution for problems of investment and development of Latin America...must involve sooner or later the creation of an Inter-American Bank" (Villaseñor, 1948, p. 192)

The shift from a hemispheric to a world view in the U.S. government, although understandable considering the expanded global role of that country, was at first baffling and then a matter of increasing concern for Latin America. After all, the Roosevelt Administration, as part of the dialogue with Latin American countries, had developed and tried in the region many of the ideas and approaches to political and economic issues that were later projected globally. Emilio Collado, a high official in the Treasury and State Departments during the Roosevelt Administration and one of the members that testified in favor of the Inter-American Bank at the Senate hearings, noted, referring to economic issues, that "a lot of these things had a Latin American initiation and spread to other parts of the world, rather than the other way around. I mean, we started programs more rapidly in Latin America than in most other places." (Oral History Interview with Emilio Collado, 1971).[34]

An example of this pattern was how the negotiations linked to the Inter-American Bank ended up being the basis for the creation of the Bretton Wood institutions (Horsefield, 1969; see also Helleiner, 2009a and 2009b). While the legislation of the Inter-American Bank was delayed in Congress, H. D. White, in 1942, started to work on a global reconstruction bank, using the ideas and structure that came from the negotiation of the regional bank. The components related to the functions of an investment bank in the Charter of the Inter-American Bank were the foundation for the creation of the World Bank. The latter included the general concept of shares held by governments, with countries having representatives at the Board of Directors and voting that would be proportional to their shares in the institution. But different from the Inter-American Bank, the World Bank was limited to project lending, did not receive deposits, and it made loans only to

---

[34] Similarly, in 1941, Berle had told to a Canadian audience that "we can no longer look at the hemisphere chopped up into economic segments, each of which endeavors to manipulate its interests against the others. In the combination of the new conception with the new mechanisms we have already gone a long way towards establishing the foundation of what will be the cooperative international economics of the future...It is not accident, in my judgment, that this has occurred in the New World. Our great contribution has been the erection of an American system within which different nations and different race groups have found it possible to live without hatred, at peace, and in smooth working relationship. We are now on the way towards making a second and equally significant contribution: the creation of a system in which economic interests of the various nations are found to be not in conflict, but in cooperation" (cited in Green, 1971, p. 82 and 83)

governments, or to private or public firms, on the basis of a government guarantee of repayment.[35] Four fifths of the subscribed capital was not paid in cash but was used as a guarantee fund against losses, which was a way of leveraging the cash contributions of the United States and other member countries. Therefore, borrowing in world markets against such guarantee, one of the possible ways of generating loanable funds contemplated in the operations of the Inter-American Bank, was now firmly established in the World Bank charter.[36]

However, other characteristics of the Inter-American Bank were not incorporated in the charter of the World Bank, such as the vast powers to conduct normal commercial banking functions.

Also, some of the functions of a Central Bank envisaged for the Inter-American Bank constituted the antecedents for the International Monetary Fund, such as assisting in stabilizing the currencies and facilitating monetary equilibrium, and providing research and technical assistance in topics of public finance, exchange rates, banking, and monetary policy.[37] As in the World Bank, shares were held by governments, and each country had a member on the board of directors and voting was proportional to the shares owned by each country. The United States was, again, the main shareholder.

In July 1944 the United Nations Monetary and Financial Conference started in Bretton Woods, New Hampshire, to discuss the possible creation of two new institutions, the International Bank for Reconstruction and Development (IBRD, later known as the World Bank) and the International Monetary Fund (IMF). Latin American

---

[35] In fact, the principal function that the founders anticipated for the World Bank was not to make direct loans (which would eventually become the main activity) but to guarantee private investments, thus facilitating the provision of capital for reconstruction in the immediate post war. In the words of then Assistant Secretary of State Dean Acheson (quoted in Dell, 1972) the World Bank would "investigate the soundness of the projects for which capital is desired, and if [the World Bank] agrees they are sound, it will guarantee loans made by private banks." (p.19)

[36] Borrowing in world markets would become the main way of funding the ordinary (i.e. market-based) operations of the multilateral development banks, as opposed to the concessional windows of these same institutions, which would need recurrent direct funding using taxpayers' money.

[37] As mentioned before, Bordo and Schwartz (2001) had shown that the 1936 Mexican loan from the Exchange Stabilization Fund was also another precedent for the IMF. A more remote precedent was the Gold Clearance Fund Convention discussed at some Pan-American meetings between 1915 and 1920. Those antecedents, using Collado's words, had a "Latin American initiation" as well.

countries saw the Bretton Woods Conference as an opportunity to receive economic support, considering that, in their opinion they had subsidized Allied efforts through the provision of commodities at controlled prices during the war.[38] The fact that the Latin American republics represented a sizable voting block at the conference, being nineteen of the forty-four countries in attendance, also seemed to support their high expectations. The Latin American countries that participated in the conference (Argentina had not been invited) fully supported the creation of the IBRD; although with more reservations, they also approved the IMF. These organizations became operational in 1946, not without another round of skirmishes with U.S. private banks that were concerned about the possible impact of the Bretton Woods institutions on their operations (see Collado 1971 and 1974).

Latin America also had high expectations about the United Nations Conference on International Organization that took place in San Francisco during April-June, 1945, and which led to the creation of the United Nations on October 24, 1945. Again, Latin American countries represented a large proportion of the participating states. As in the case of Woodrow Wilson with the League of Nations, several of the ideas for the United Nations had been discussed first in the context of the U.S.-Latin America relations, especially by Sumner Welles.[39] Latin American countries were concerned that the Security Council, in which they did not have a seat, could make decisions about their security issues and wanted to keep regional arrangements separate. The U.S. government, on the other hand, with the focus already turned towards world issues, did not want regional considerations to intrude

---

[38] Stephen Rabe (1988) mentioned that during the war "Latin America made a $3 billion non-interest-bearing loan to the United States and could not collect on the principal" (p.16 and 17). He also quotes former President from Costa Rica, José Figueres, who estimated that by selling coffee at controlled prices, the country lost about half of four coffee crops during the war. Villaseñor (1948) also refers to the Latin American losses because of sales of raw materials to the United States at controlled prices.

[39] Sumner Welles, who became a close advisor to President Roosevelt, had built his diplomatic career in Latin America, starting with the Wilson Administration. Some historians credit Welles with being the architect of the United Nations, as Roosevelt had given him a "dominance over U.N. planning" that had "started to embitter Hull" (Stephen C. Schlesinger, 2003, p. 41). The rivalry between Welles and Secretary of State Hull ended with the resignation of the former, after he suffered political attacks related to a sexual scandal. Hull eventually received the Nobel Peace Prize for the creation of the United Nations.

into U.N. arrangements. The United States was concerned that any special arrangement for the Americas could be used both by the Soviet Union to strengthen its control over Eastern Europe and by the United Kingdom and other European countries to maintain their colonies and spheres of influence.

In the end, Latin American countries got the inclusion in the U.N. Charter of an exception for what the Security Council could do in regards to the regional security agreement embedded in the Chapultepec Act that had been approved earlier that year (see below). Latin America achieved that diplomatic victory working with members of the U.S. delegation, such as Senator Vanderberg and Assistant Secretary of State for American Affairs, Nelson Rockefeller, who were more sympathetic to the idea of maintaining greater hemispheric collaboration (although for different reasons).

While the San Francisco Conference left Latin countries with at least the regional security exception, the Bretton Woods Conference, on the other hand, basically preempted for several years the emergence of a financial institution only for Latin America.

In 1944 and 1945 it was becoming increasingly clear that the United States, to the dismay of the Latin American republics, had moved to a global view in which the importance of the region was greatly diminished. The U.S. government considered that Latin America had escaped the conflict relatively unscathed. Even if Latin American protests for having had to sell commodities at low prices were accepted, the United States saw itself suffering more in human and economic terms because of the war. On the other hand, from the perspective of the Latin American countries it has also been argued that a) the war effort shifted the economic structure of the region again towards primary products; b) the limits of U.S. exports of consumer goods to the region fuelled domestic inflation in Latin America; and c) inflationary pressures after World War II eroded the value of the reserves in dollars held by countries in the region (Green, 1971). But the United States considered that the region was going to benefit from the multilateral institutions already created and from the restoration of economic activity in Europe, which would buy Latin American exports and sell consumer goods to the region.[40] These contrasting views

---

[40] The war years also saw a significant rise of development finance institutions in the region, which, in many cases, were established with capital from the Export-Import Bank (Nyhart, 1968). By the end of the war, 80 percent of the development finance

would frame much of the subsequent interaction between Latin America and the United States, particularly in economic matters. Eventually, in 1947 President Truman withdrew the Inter-American Bank Convention from Congress, with the Bretton Woods institutions already approved. The Cold War opened a new strategic setting.

---

institutions in the then-developing world were in Latin America, with the word "fomento" appearing in the titles of the new entities. The approach was pioneered by Peru's Banco de Fomento Agropecuario and later used by the "Corporaciones de Fomento" from Chile, Bolivia and Venezuela, among others (Nyhart, 1968).

Fourth Phase

The Cold War and the Inter-American Development Bank

a) The Cold War in Latin America and the Early Predominance of Security Approaches

With the end of World War II and the emergence of the Soviet Union as the main strategic competitor, in the late 1940s U.S. attention shifted further away from Latin America. The main structural geopolitical challenge for the United States was far away from the Americas: it consisted in the strategic vacuum along the frontiers of the Soviet Union, in Europe, Middle East, and Asia. Old Russian enemies, such as Germany and Japan, had been defeated, and others, such as the United Kingdom, France, and China, were weakened by the war or internal problems. The Soviet Union, although also affected by the war, still had a stronger military presence in the region and was willing to move into that vacuum to establish what the Soviets saw as a legitimate perimeter of defense. The United States, in contrast, considered any such maneuver as a threat to world geopolitical balances and an expression of communist expansionism. The large differences in economic and political systems between both countries were, at minimum, a source of misunderstandings. More often than not, they led to direct confrontations.

Across the geographical arc that enveloped the Soviet Union, the main threat, from the perspective of the United States, centered on Europe. The Truman Doctrine of 1947 that promised help to countries resisting communist advances focused on the deteriorating political situation in Turkey and Greece. In that year several initiatives were launched for Europe such as the Marshall Plan and the program for European integration. Also, the General Agreement on Tariffs and Trade (GATT) was established to ensure that the protectionist trade wars that worsened the Great Depression would not happen again. But, to the disappointment of many Latin American countries, agriculture was excluded from GATT disciplines. This exclusion consolidated a pattern of agricultural protectionism and subsidies in rich countries that began to be slowly redressed only with the Uruguay Round, completed about a half century later in 1994.

At the same time, in the immediate aftermath of World War II there was a flourishing of democratic participation and institutions in Latin America, which included the presence of communist parties. Labor unions expanded in the region and the notion of the defense of democracy extended from support to the Allies to the need of greater social participation. However, by 1947-48 a Cold War mindset began to consolidate. Dominant groups in Latin America started to worry about the political advances of the labor movements and of the political parties from the left. Cold War concerns about Soviet influence in the Americas soon eclipsed other objectives related to democracy and economic development in the region (Smith, 1999; Rabe, 1988).

The Inter-American Conference on Problems of War and Peace (March, 1945 in Mexico) approved the Inter-American Reciprocal Assistance and Solidarity Act (Act of Chapultepec). This document defined "a regional arrangement for dealing with such matters relating to the maintenance of international peace and security as are appropriate for regional action in this Hemisphere." The text of the Act also clarified that "said arrangement, and the pertinent activities and procedures, shall be consistent with the purposes and principles of the general international organization, when established" (Inter-American Conference on Problems of War and Peace, 1948). As mentioned already, during the U.N. Conference in San Francisco that took place a few months after this meeting, Latin American countries succeeded in protecting the regional arrangement by including specific language in Article 51 of the Charter of the United Nations.

The next inter-American meeting (Conference for the Maintenance of Continental Peace and Security), took place in Rio de Janeiro, on August 15-September 2, 1947, and led to the Rio Treaty of 1947. This agreement served as a model for other regional pacts, such as the 1949 North Atlantic Treaty, a military alliance with Europe that established a system of collective defense and created the North Atlantic Treaty Organization (NATO).

The 1945 and 1947 Inter-American Conferences did not discuss economic issues and focused basically on security matters, although the United States suggested an Economic Charter of the Americas in Mexico 1945. The proposed Charter proved to be controversial mainly because, regarding industrialization, the United States' proposal opposed public interventions to help domestic producers. On the other hand, the document also asserted, among other things, that "poverty, under-nutrition or lack of health" in any of the countries would affect all of them.

In general, economic discrepancies in the Americas continued along familiar lines. Latin American countries felt that they had helped the war effort with cheap raw materials and, in some cases, with troops, and that they had supported the United States in the creation of the Bretton Woods institutions and the United Nations. Yet, notwithstanding such support, they had been left with little influence in the newly created international system and were not receiving the same economic aid from the United States that other regions were getting.

U.S. officials, in turn, argued that the main war effort, in human and materials, had been borne by the United States; that Latin America, which had suffered less, both in economic and human terms, also benefitted from the more open world created after World War II; and private investments plus support from the Bretton Woods institutions and the Export-Import Bank, were enough to finance the development of the Southern neighbors.

The Ninth Inter-American Conference took place in Bogota (March 30-May 2 1948). It marked the transition from the Pan-American Union to the newly created Organization of American States (OAS). The conference also approved the Declaration of the Rights and Duties of Man, the first international human rights instrument. In the economic sphere, the Inter-American Economic and Social Council (CIES in Spanish), which had been created as the successor to the Inter-American Economic and Financial and Economic Advisory Committee, became one of the permanent organs of the OAS under provisions of the 1948 charter.[41]

---

[41] The Conference recognized that "the functions attributed to the Economic Commission of Latin America (ECLA), which was created by the United Nations Economic and Social Council on February 25 1948, are strikingly similar to those of the CIES" and that therefore it was "essential to avoid any duplication of functions amongst organizations." Raúl Prebisch and his allies in the U.N. system had to work hard first to create and then to sustain ECLA, which was constantly under the threat of elimination due to the alleged duplication of functions but, mainly, because of the

During the conference it was clear that several Latin American countries were displeased with the bilateralism of the Export-Import Bank and with what they considered the stringent conditions and unresponsiveness of the IMF and the World Bank.[42] The latter was also criticized for its exclusive focus on specific projects and the neglect of more comprehensive economy-wide programs.

The debate focused again on the creation of a regional financial institution and several proposals were made regarding the composition and purpose of the institution to be created: Mexico suggested a revision of the statutes of the Inter-American Bank of 1940, while Venezuela advocated the creation of a Development Corporation, emphasizing the importance of technical cooperation for the preparation of sound projects (Broide, 1961). Consequently, the CIES was asked to conduct a study on "the possibility and suitability of an Inter-American Bank or an Inter-American Development Corporation or both" (Comas, 2000).

The staff of the CIES prepared in 1949 a report presenting the pros and cons of creating a regional financial institution, but without giving an opinion. Eventually in a special session of the CIES in March-April 1950, the idea of a regional institution was discussed but did not have enough support, particularly given the opposition from the United States. The proposal was temporarily shelved (Broide, 1961).

On the political front, there was a growing debate in the Americas about whether the presence of communist parties was a threat to democracy. Conservative circles in the United States and Latin America were increasingly concerned about what they perceived as the communist threat in labor unions of key industries such as oil, copper, and sugar. The global contest with the Soviet Union appeared to have moved to the domestic political arena, where some dominant

---

resistance in some circles about the development theories advanced by Prebisch (Dosman, 2008). Years later, ECLA would include a "C" for Caribbean in its acronym, becoming ECLAC.

[42] The World Bank's fixation with earning a "hard-headed banker" reputation necessarily entailed stringent conditions, but the issue of political influences on the decision-making process was also important. For instance, the provision in the World Bank Charter about avoiding political considerations in the approval of loans was interpreted by John McCloy, President of the World Bank from March 1947 to June 1949, as meaning that there would be no "loans that were inconsistent with American foreign policy" (Kapur, Lewis and Webb, 1997).

economic and social groups in Latin American countries began to look with concern at different developments that they perceived as threatening their established positions.

At the same time, Prebisch's ideas about the asymmetries between core and peripheral countries gained ground. Countries that had embarked in efforts to industrialize their economies felt vindicated by his electrifying presentation at the first ECLA meeting in Havana in 1949, where Prebisch focused on the problems and potential solutions for the development of Latin America (Dosman, 2008).

At the same time, a change in the economic structure was under way in many Latin American countries, particularly the larger ones, with the expansion of industrial production. Increasing rural-urban migration and widening income disparities were fertile ground for social tensions. Those changes, along with the expansion of democracy, were significantly transforming the social and political landscape in many countries of the region. There was a general tendency towards political liberalization, which, pushed by the advance of labor unions, led to social demands and advances in progressive legislation (Bethel and Roxborough, 1988).

There were also important transformations at the global level. By 1949, the Soviet Union had completed the first atomic test and the Communists won control in China over the Nationalists, starting a "red scare" in the United States. In 1950 Paul Nitze drafted the secret U.S. policy document NSC 68 that codified the doctrine of containment of Communism. It was approved by Truman that year.

Concerned with global affairs and the advance of the Soviet Union, the Truman Administration analyzed Latin America basically in the context of the wider containment policy and focused basically on free trade and military aid to help the region. Truman's Point Four doctrine became the foundation for U.S. international aid programs. Those programs, however, largely bypassed Latin America as it was deemed politically stable.[43] However, the fact that the number of

---

[43] In his inaugural speech on January 20, 1949, President Truman presented as a fourth objective of foreign policy (hence the name Point Four) the need to make "the benefits of our scientific advances and industrial progress available for the improvement and growth of underdeveloped areas," arguing that the fact that more than half the people of the world were living in poverty constituted a threat "both to them and to more prosperous areas." The new program would offer to less-advanced countries U.S. scientific and technical knowledge (which Truman argued was abundant) rather than material resources (which he considered more limited).

dictatorships in Latin America was increasing clearly indicated that discontent was growing in the region.

At the same time, the U.S. prescription for the development of Latin America based solely on private capital contrasted with the approaches applied in other regions. ECLA was hardly the only advocate of more active government participation and economic aid to reduce developmental imbalances: the Marshall Plan and New Deal initiatives such as the Tennessee Valley Authority, all popularized the virtues of public sector planning. The expansion of national income accounting and other economic and social data, which facilitated the use of empirical analyses of societies and nations, laid the ground for what was called "modernization theory." There were growing expectations among social scientists and policy makers about the possibility of an orderly transformation of traditional societies. Some economists suggested "big push" approaches to development based on economic aid for capital-intensive projects. The wave of decolonization sweeping across the globe provided both opportunities to try these ideas and created the risk that the Soviet Union would influence the direction of this debate.

The economic and political trends in Latin America were already pointing to the convergence of U.S. security worries about the region with the permanent yearning of the countries in the region for economic and social development. That combination of security and development concerns would eventually lead to the creation of the Inter-American Development Bank, but by the end of the Truman Administration and the first term of President Eisenhower that convergence had not yet been recognized by U.S. decision makers.

In January 1953 the Eisenhower Administration began with a strategic vision that changed the principles of Truman's containment policy, considered to be too costly in economic terms and which appeared to leave in the hands of the Soviet Union the initiative regarding where to put pressure on the Western alliance.[44] The new approach was based on asymmetric responses, utilizing atomic power, reducing the costs of conventional forces and resorting to covert

---

[44] Some of the more conservative critics of Truman, such as John Foster Dulles who later became Secretary of State in the Eisenhower Administration, considered containment also immoral because the only acceptable policy against the Soviets and communism was one of rolling them back, and not only containing them. The latter approach was strongly rejected by Dulles and other critics because it seemed to condone Communist control over certain countries and areas.

operations. The United States also signed a series of reciprocal defense treaties, mostly with countries in the periphery of the Soviet Union.

A staunch believer in private enterprise as a solution to Latin America's problems, Eisenhower objected to the provision of economic aid. When a report penned by his brother Milton convinced Assistant Secretary of State John Moors Cabot to push for more support for the region, the Republican Party quickly dismissed the idea and Cabot was quietly transferred to a European embassy (Rabe, 1988).

However, Secretary of State John Foster Dulles started to fear that the frequent fluctuations in Latin American economic fortunes would be fertile soil for the advance of Communism. Therefore, although his main objective in the upcoming Inter-American Conference programmed for Caracas in 1954 was to persuade the Southern republics to sign an anti-communist resolution, Dulles also secured Eisenhower's approval to make two economic announcements. First, there was going to be more Export-Import Bank credits for the region.[45] Second, the United States would support an economic conference in the Americas that the Latin countries had been requesting since the 1945 Inter-American Conference in Mexico (Rabe, 1988, particularly p.69).

The Tenth Inter-American Conference in Caracas (March 1-28, 1954) issued the "Declaration of Solidarity for the Preservation of the Political Integrity of the American States against International Communist Intervention." It was agreed that "the domination or control of the political institutions of any American State by the international communist movement…would constitute a threat to the sovereignty and political independence of the American States, endangering the peace of America, and would call for a meeting of consultation to consider the adoption of appropriate action" (Organization of American States, 1954).

Besides the anti-communist declaration, in Caracas it was also decided that the Economic Ministers would meet in Rio de Janeiro by the end of 1954, with the objective of trying to find "practical solutions to the problems that affect Latin American economic and social development." The Economic Commission for Latin America,

---

[45] When the Eisenhower Administration took office, the longer-term developmental loans of the Export-Import Bank to the region that had been promoted under the Roosevelt and Truman Administrations were significantly scaled down. This decision was reversed in order to have something to offer at the Caracas Conference (Rabe, 1988).

which had already established its presence in the region under the leadership of Raul Prebisch, was asked to help prepare the meeting.

The general socio-economic background in Latin American countries for that meeting was changing. Although at the beginning of the 1950s the region showed high rates of economic growth, after the end of the Korean War in 1953 the economic situation in Latin America deteriorated. Prices of agricultural commodities declined in world markets. The United States, the main economic partner of the region, entered into a recession in mid-1953 that lasted until mid-1954.[46] All these developments affected negatively Latin American exports and terms of trade, leading to balance of payments and fiscal problems in the region. Most of the Latin American countries suffered declines in income per capital either in 1953 or 1954, while social unrest increased. The fact that at the time the region appeared to be the only one not receiving economic aid from the United States was adding to a growing sense of disenchantment with their powerful neighbor among Latin American countries.

While the region was asking for economic support to foster development, the thinking in Washington continued to go in a different direction. For instance, the Eisenhower-appointed Randall Commission on Foreign Economic Policy clarified the Administration's stance bluntly: "Underdeveloped areas are claiming a right to economic aid from the United States…We recognize no such right" (Randall Commission on Foreign Economic Policy, 1954, page 9). A congressional mission visiting fifteen countries in the region at the beginning of 1954 upon returning to Washington reported that "South America…is populated by friendly people who want to become closely identified with the United States culturally, politically, and economically" (Jackson, 1954). Such rosy vision contrasted with the fact that classified security briefs to the president were reporting increasing dissatisfaction in the region.

---

[46] According to Dosman (2008), in the early 1950s about 50 percent of imports and 48 percent of exports of Latin America were with the United States. The region was important for the United States as well, considering that, in addition to the strong trade links, U.S. investments were twice those in Asia and larger than in Western Europe and Canada (Dosman, 2008; p. 289). In his detailed work on Prebisch, Dosman (2008) quotes a U.S. State Department official arguing that "Latin America is our largest customer, supplier and field of foreign investment" and also "an indispensable and irreplaceable ally" (Dosman, 2008; p. 525). Latin American countries were also aware of those facts, and, therefore, were even more baffled by what they perceived as lack of U.S. interest for the region.

It should be noted too that by 1954-55 the previous democratic advances in the region after World War II had been stopped and, in several countries, reversed. The last democratic retreat had been the military coup against the government of President Jacobo Arbenz in Guatemala. He was toppled in June 1954 with support from covert operations by the Eisenhower Administration, who feared Soviet influence in Arbenz's cabinet. Most Latin American countries criticized strongly the U.S. intervention and even the respected OAS Secretary General at that time, Alberto Lleras Camargo, resigned in protest.

These two different views about what were the main challenges in the region were going to clash in the coming economic Ministerial meeting in Rio de Janeiro.

b) The Slow Reemergence of the Idea of a Regional Bank: the Quitandinha, Santiago, and Buenos Aires Meetings

As agreed in Caracas, the Meeting of the Ministers of Economy took place at the Hotel Quitandinha in Rio, between November 22 and December 2, 1954. Before the meeting there was a strong interdepartmental debate within the Eisenhower Administration (Rabe, 1988). On the one hand, the agency that managed U.S. economic assistance (the Foreign Operations Administration, FOA), with support from the CIA and the Department of Defense, which were increasingly concerned about security challenges in the region, advocated economic support for Latin America, including the possibility of creating a regional bank, and proposed some help to stabilize prices of commodities. On the other side of the debate, the U.S. Treasury, under the direction of George Humphrey, a fiscal conservative and strong believer in free markets, advised self-reliance, free trade, and private investments as the way to help develop Latin American countries. The disagreements clearly emerged in a meeting with the president. In this debate Eisenhower basically sided with Humphrey, who was going to head the U.S. delegation to Río.[47] As a concession to those concerned about economic problems in Latin America, it was agreed that the Export-Import Bank could further expand its operations in the region and the overall lending capacity of the institution would also be raised.

---

[47] Eisenhower, however, chided Humphrey reminding him that the "United States was not merely doing 'business' in Latin America, but was fighting a war there against Communism" (Rabe, 1988, p.71).

Humphrey also wanted Latin American support for the creation of the International Finance Corporation, the private sector arm of the World Bank (Broide, 1961; Rabe, 1988).

On the Latin American side, the preparation was mostly handled by ECLA. Under the coordination and guidance of Prebisch, a commission of six experts from Latin America was organized. ECLA prepared a background document entitled "International Cooperation for a Latin American Development Policy" (Broide, 1968; Dosman, 2008).[48] It was based on the thesis advanced in the first ECLA meeting in Havana in 1949, by then widely accepted in Latin America, but not by the U.S. government, about the deterioration of the terms of trade and the need to move away from specialization in primary products and step up support for industrialization.

The document suggested the creation of a regional development bank and the need to ensure 1,000 million dollars per year (or about 8,000 million dollars in March 2010 money) in development finance, particularly for industrialization. Those funds would come from different sources, including the proposed new institution, the private sector, the World Bank, and the Export-Import Bank.[49] The new regional institution (with the tentative name of Inter-American Fund for the Development of Industry, Agriculture, and Mining) would have a capital of 250 million dollars (about 2,000 million dollars in March 2010 money), paid equally by the United States and Latin American countries. Only 20 percent of the capital would be paid in cash, while the rest would act as a standing guarantee to be called only if needed. The institution could borrow in global financial markets. The proposal also contemplated an annual and separate contribution of 50 million dollars during a period of fifteen years (or a total of 750 million dollars) only from the United States. ECLA's document also included measures to strengthen economic planning, stabilize commodity prices, improve domestic taxation, and promote agrarian reform (Broide, 1961; Dosman, 2008).

During the conference the delegates from Latin America complained about the low level of financing to the region from the

---

[48] That commission included two members, Eduardo Frei from Chile and Carlos Lleras Restrepo from Colombia, who would later become Presidents of their respective countries.
[49] According to the proposal, 600-650 million dollars would come from the Export-Import Bank and the World Bank; 50-100 million dollars from the regional institution; and the rest from the private sector (Broide, 1961).

World Bank and the Export-Import Bank. They also criticized the operations of these institutions because, among other things, they did not consider financing local costs and social projects, and funded isolated projects instead of whole development programs.[50] The Chilean delegation (one of whose members was Felipe Herrera who later became IDB's first president) presented a proposal for the creation of a regional financial institution (an Inter-American Banking System). In that scheme, the Central Banks in the region would pool 1,000 million dollars of their reserves (estimated by the Chilean document at 3,500 million dollars, or about 28,000 millions in March 2010 money) and use those funds to finance development projects in the member countries. The institution could also receive deposits from other sources, and issue its own debt in global markets. This proposal, which was different from ECLA's, evoked some resistances: for instance, the Mexican delegation raised concerns about the legal implications of using reserves for purposes other than those contemplated in the Central Banks' respective charters. Still, Chile, Colombia, Ecuador, and Haiti presented a joint project along those lines, and suggested the creation of a Commission to analyze the idea (Broide, 1961).

Representing the United States at the conference, Secretary Humphrey stated that his country lacked the money necessary to finance such a bank; that Latin America should instead use more effectively existing institutions; and that private, not public, funding should underpin development. Therefore the United States, accompanied by Peru, abstained, when the rest of the countries agreed to create a "Committee of Experts," which in six months had to develop a plan for a regional financial organization and present it to the Organization of American States. [51] [52]

---

[50] The economic thinking at that time was that the problem that affected developing countries was the lack of hard currency to finance the imported component of the investments required to sustain economic growth. In consequence, loans from the existing financing institutions covered only those imported goods and services. Locally sourced goods and services could be paid with the domestic currency and, therefore, were not financed by the World Bank or the Export-Import Bank.

[51] Apparently the delegate from Argentina, Antonio Cafiero, whose Government was at that time trying to improve relations with the United States, had received instructions to vote with this country. Therefore, Argentina would have had to abstain as well. However, seeing the strong interest from most Latin American countries in the creation of the regional bank, the Argentine delegate decided to ignore the instructions and voted in favor of the idea of creating the Committee of

Secretary Humphrey also rejected most of the other economic proposals discussed at the conference, because, according to the official U.S. view, they implied excessive interference of the government in the operation of the markets (what was called "economic nationalism").

Clearly, the United States and the Latin American countries approached the Quitandinha Conference with very different perspectives. Although Humphrey gave a positive account of the conference to Eisenhower, the meeting was considered a failure by most participants, including some in the U.S. delegation (Rabe, 1988; Dosman, 2008). The Latin American countries had nonetheless succeeded in putting forward an integrated agenda for development based on ECLA's ideas. The whole episode increased both the distrust of the Eisenhower Administration for ECLA and the respect for Prebisch and his group in Latin America. Many of the proposals would reappear a few years later, when deteriorating economic conditions in Latin America and the fateful trip to the region by Vice-President Richard Nixon prompted a reassessment of Latin American policies within the Eisenhower Administration. But that was still four years away.

As approved in Quitandinha, the Committee of Experts from Latin America countries only, met in Santiago from February 17 to April 15, 1955.[53] There was a general agreement among the delegates about the causes of dissatisfaction with the international financial institutions existing at that time. The criticisms mentioned included: the limited volume of funding; the existing restrictions on lending to countries because they were considered -by those international financial institutions- unable to service debt; limits on loans for some purposes (with arguments such as the narrowness of domestic markets; lack of technical ability to manage a company; that the project increased supply in markets with already excessive global production; and so on); lack of financing in local currency; the condition that funds

---

Experts. His position was ratified by Argentina's President, Juan Perón, when, upon his return home, Antonio Cafiero explained the reasons for his vote (personal communication with Antonio Cafiero).

[52] The commission had experts from the Central Banks in Argentina, Brazil, Chile, Colombia, Cuba, Costa Rica, Mexico, Venezuela, and Haiti, and a representative from ECLA.

[53] The discussion of the meeting in what follows is based on the detailed account by Broide (1961).

be used to buy products and services only from certain countries; excessive requirements in terms of guarantees, or negotiations of previous debts; short tenor of the loans; and high interest rates (Broide, 1961).[54]

Another main argument to support the creation of a regional bank was the low level of representation of Latin American countries in the existing financial institutions, which was considered the basic reason why the decision-making system in those organizations ignored regional realities and aspirations. Countries in Latin America expected that a new regional institution had a more adequate participation of the developing countries and a more direct knowledge of the developmental problems of the region. The new institution was expected to complement the international financial system and, at the same time, promote cooperation among the countries of Latin America and the Caribbean. The countries in the region also argued that to the extent that the demand for financing was higher than the supply (which the Latin American representatives considered to be the obvious case), the potential duplication of some activities with the existing international financial institutions was not a good reason against the creation of the new regional bank.

The group of experts in Santiago drafted a proposal for the creation of the new institution and defined its objective as the promotion of economic development through facilitation of investments in public, private or mixed ventures. This not only included financing projects that would generate direct income to pay back the loans, but also infrastructural and social projects that tried to improve production or the quality of life in different ways. For

---

[54] International financial organizations are obliged by their Charters to consider the possibility of repayment when approving loans (this is true today; the Charter of the IDB, for instance, includes that requirement to process operations; see Article III, Section 7 (a) (iii)). The problem as seen by Latin American countries was the long list of criteria, many subjective or politically oriented, that the existing financial institutions applied to decide whether to lend or not. In this regard, Broide (1961) mentions, citing a study by Raymond Mikesell, also part of the technical documents commissioned by the OAS, those criteria: "internal political stability; country's attitude regarding external obligations; internal economic organization and stage of economic progress of the country; structure of foreign trade; perspectives of balance of payment, and economic and financial policies" (p.41). Obviously, this allowed great latitude to approve or reject loans to countries according to the political preferences of the main shareholders in the existing institutions, something that Latin American countries wanted to correct in the new regional institution.

instance, projects such as water and sanitation generated positive, although indirect, economic effects. The suggested bank would also consider projects denominated in local currency and would provide long-term financing.

Therefore, the proposal tried to address many of the criticisms that Latin American countries had been voicing about the credit policies of the existing international financial institutions and allowed types of operations and facilities that had not been implemented by those institutions up to that time.

Authorized capital was proposed to be 200 million dollars (somewhat more than 1,600 million dollars in March 2010 currency), 50 percent of which would be paid when the bank was constituted and 50 percent as a guarantee for future commitments. One third of the capital was to be subscribed by the United States (an aspiration only, considering that this country did not participate in the meeting) and two thirds by Latin America. New subscriptions would be permitted as long as they were approved by three fourths of votes. The shares for each country would be determined by their participation at the IMF.[55]

The new entity would have broad coverage in its operations, and the future management would be granted flexibility in its functions, with the only limitation that resources were to be used with a developmental objective. In many senses the proposed institution, like the 1940 Inter-American Bank, had functions of a commercial bank, an investment bank, and even a Central Bank. As a commercial bank it was allowed to receive deposits, take loans, discount its portfolio, provide short term loans and execute short term investments. It would also operate as an investment bank by issuing its own debt instruments to fund loans and investments with medium and long term maturities, and by acting as an agent and coordinator between firms and investors in the Americas. As a Central Bank, it could be the financial agent of the equivalent national institutions in Latin America and of governments and public entities.

In spite of this ample range of operations, the bank was explicitly excluded from offering budget-support loans (i.e. global amounts to cover public sector expenditures without specification of the use of the funds), a point that was also raised in the context of the 1940 Inter-American Bank (see Villaseñor, 1941). Another issue that generated a

---

[55] Argentina, which was not a member of the IMF at that time, was assigned the same participation as Brazil (Argentina joined the IMF in September, 1956).

long debate was the idea, proposed by Chile in Quitandinha, of using part of the reserves of the Central Banks as a source of funding for the new institution. This idea faced resistance and was eventually discarded.

The draft charter for the institution included other covenants such as the right of each country to block any operation in its territory if the government objected to it, and stated that the bank could not impose the condition to use the proceeds from loans to buy goods or services in any specific country (thus addressing another of the Latin American criticisms to the then existing financial institutions).

The difference in voting power, with Latin American countries subscribing a majority of the shares, was a distinctive aspect of the governance structure. Other than that, the new institution was structured as the existing multilateral financial organizations. The General Board was designated as the supreme authority, with representatives from the member countries. The voting system at the General Board was similar to the one suggested for the 1940 Inter-American Bank and then implemented at the IMF and the World Bank: there was a fixed percentage of votes for each member plus an additional vote for each subscribed share. None of the shareholders could exceed 33 percent of votes. Additionally, there would be a Board of Directors which would include the President of the bank and six Directors. The President of the bank and three of the Directors would be designated by the General Board while one of the other three Directors would be chosen by the main shareholder and the other two by the rest of the member countries. Both the President and the Directors would have a mandate of two years and could be reelected indefinitely.

The Board of Directors would have the authority to establish reserves and to impose global limits to the volume of operations; study and approve loan applications; approve borrowing or issuing of debt by the bank; and set the interest rates and fees to be charged. The President would be in charge of managing the bank's ordinary business under the supervision of the Board of Directors.

The document prepared by the Commission of Experts with the proposed charter for the regional bank was presented to the Inter-American Economic and Social Council of the OAS in June 1955, and from there it was sent to the member countries for consideration. The work by the experts in Santiago had been careful and far-reaching. Many options for funding, operations, structure and decision-making of the proposed institution had been thoroughly debated, adopting some of them and discarding others. The bank's charter that emerged from Santiago represented a serious and realistic proposal for an institution that addressed Latin American concerns about development finance for the region. In fact, several elements of the institutional and operational architecture suggested would eventually find its way in the Charter of the IDB.

However, the response from Latin American countries was discouraging. Out of the nine countries that participated in the Santiago meeting, three did not answer the request for consideration of the proposal (Argentina, Haiti, and Venezuela); one of them voted against it (Cuba, because some of its suggestions had not been included); another one declared that it had not finished with the assessment (Brazil); and only four of them gave their support (Chile, Colombia, Costa Rica, and Mexico). However, five countries that did not participate in the Commission of Experts voted favorably (Dominican Republic, El Salvador, Honduras, Panama, and Ecuador). But this support was insufficient considering that, according to the proposed Charter, at least 50 percent of the subscribed capital was required to create the new institution. In fact, the tepid to negative answer to the proposal was based on the fact that the United States was not supporting the creation of the new institution, and that there were doubts that it could function as envisaged without the participation of that country.

The project was shelved, although new proposals emerged after the 1956 meeting of the presidents of the Americas in Panama, where they gathered to celebrate the 130th anniversary of the First Panama Congress called by Simón Bolívar. One of the decisions was to organize a commission of presidential delegates to look at the welfare of the peoples of the Americas. In the meetings of those delegates the issue of a regional financial institution reappeared (there were specific proposals from Chile, Cuba, and Venezuela), with Latin and U.S. delegates basically reiterating the same divergent positions (Broide, 1961). Those ideas were once more sent to the appropriate OAS bodies to be studied further.

Therefore, the topic of the regional bank was again discussed in 1957 at the OAS Economic Conference in Buenos Aires, just as unrest was increasing in the region. However, global events had been focusing the attention of the Eisenhower Administration away from Latin America: there have been skirmishes with China related to the

Quemoy- Matsu islands in 1954/5; the Soviet Union detonated the first full-powered hydrogen bomb in 1955; and there were expanding conflicts in the Middle East, particularly in Egypt with the construction of the Aswan Dam and the conflict over Suez in 1956. The 1957 Eisenhower Doctrine, which centered on the Middle East, argued for the use of armed forces in response to imminent or actual Soviet aggression as well as the provision of aid for the countries opposed to Communism. The launching of the first inter-continental ballistic missile by the Soviet Union in August 1957 and the Sputnik in October 1957 generated grave concerns in the United States about losing the "space race," although that country would manage to catch up in 1958 with the launching of the Explorer 1 (in January) and Pioneer 1 (in October).

Meanwhile, Latin American countries noticed that, after the Treaty of Rome (1957), the European Economic Community had offered aid to associated countries and Africa, and wondered whether the United States would follow the example in the region (Dell, 1972).

The Economic Conference of the OAS in Buenos Aires (August 15-September 4, 1957) was supposed to be the opportunity to negotiate an inter-American economic treaty to complement the Rio Treaty and the OAS charter (Rabe, 1988, p. 95). Besides the participation of Latin American countries and the United States, there was a large representation of countries from outside the region, mostly, but not only, European.[56]

All these efforts notwithstanding, the U.S. perception continued to be that the problems in Latin America were mainly political and that the developmental problems could be solved by investments and financing from the private sector, the Export-Import Bank, and the Bretton Woods institutions. The United States also preferred to channel economic assistance through bilateral arrangements that allowed a closer control of the use of funds. The Eisenhower Administration resisted any regional organization that would require the United States to be the sole or majority funder and instead

---

[56] The countries from the Americas included Argentina, Bolivia, Brazil, Colombia, Costa Rica, Cuba, Chile, Ecuador, El Salvador, Guatemala, Haiti, Honduras, Mexico, Nicaragua, Panama, Paraguay, Peru, Dominican Republic, the United States, Uruguay and Venezuela. Participants from outside the region included Germany, Belgium, Denmark, Spain, Finland, France, England, Greece, India, Israel, Italy, Japan, Norway, Poland, Portugal, Switzerland, Yugoslavia. Canada participated as observer.

emphasized Latin America's own responsibility in fostering economic and social development.

During the conference, attended briefly by the new Treasury Secretary, Robert Anderson, the United States attached nineteen separate reservations to the 45 articles of the draft treaty, usually reinforcing a message in support of free trade and private investment (Rabe, 1988). Some U.S. high officials, including then Undersecretary of State for Economic Affairs Douglas Dillon, were reportedly unhappy with the way the requests from the Latin American countries were rejected (a pattern similar to what had happened with Secretary of the Treasury George Humphrey at Quitandinha in 1954) and returned from the conference with heightened concerns about the difficult situation in the region (Rabe, 1988).

In the end, the conference agreed to a watered-down "Economic Declaration of Buenos Aires" and to the declaration for "Financial and Economic Development," which referred to the 1954 Quitandinha resolution and the need to study ways to expand development financing. It was again recommended that once the Inter-American Economic and Social Council finished the study, it should inform the member governments so they could take appropriate action.

The U.S. position on economic aid for developing countries in general was being challenged by other events. The Communist Party Congress of 1956 had decided to reduce the military aspects of the Cold War and, instead, to compete in economic terms for the allegiance of the peoples of the developing word. In fact, early that year the Soviet Union had made diplomatic offers that would expand financial, trade, and cultural ties with Latin American countries. Bilateral commercial flows were clearly expanding after those announcements (Rabe, 1988). These developments were followed with concern by the Eisenhower Administration. The Cold War had moved now also to the economic front and was pushing the United States into a growing competition to boost longer-term economic assistance programs.

Another aspect of the on-going policy reassessment in the United States regarding Latin America was an increased realization of the need to support democratic governments, a standpoint long advocated in circles close to the Administration but that had been largely ignored.[57]

---

[57] Milton Eisenhower, the President's brother, and a personal advisor and envoy to Latin America had traveled extensively the region and written his first report in 1954

While these issues were debated in Washington, the economic situation in Latin America had deteriorated significantly during the late 1950s: while the average growth of income per capita had been about 3.5 percent during 1955-57, it declined to 1.4 percent in 1958, and turned negative in 1959 (about -1 percent).[58] These results were highly influenced by the U.S. recession that had started in mid 1957, and that from peak to bottom would led to a decline of somewhat more than 3 percent in the GDP, the largest annual drop since 1945, when World War II ended.

Yet, even in this context, Latin American demands might not have been addressed had not been for the difficult South American tour of Vice-President Nixon in May 1958. It then became evident that the United States had underestimated the extent of economic problems and social unrest in the region. Similarly, growing resentment against what was perceived as indifference towards Latin America's problems was also more acute than U.S. authorities had realized. Nixon's trip to the region prompted a drastic reversal in U.S. policies towards Latin America during Eisenhower's second term and paved the way for Kennedy's Alliance for Progress. In fact, although Kennedy's initiative with the Alliance for Progress is frequently considered the start of a different approach towards Latin America, the underlying assumptions and approaches had been established by the end of the second Eisenhower administration, which, in turn, implied, to a significant extent, the acceptance of the Quitandinha program presented by ECLA (see Rabe, 1988, and Dosman, 2008).

c) Nixon's Trip in 1958: A Wake-up Call for Hemispheric Cooperation

Initially, Nixon was only going to participate in the inauguration of Argentina's recently elected president, Arturo Frondizi, on May 1, 1958. The tour was later expanded to several countries in South America, during a period of two-and-a-half weeks. The change in the original program was an attempt by the Eisenhower Administration to

---

linking industrialization and democracy, and concluded that the absence of both was a security threat to the United States. This and later reports with similar arguments were filed without comment.

[58] This is the average for GDP per capita growth for twenty-three *individual* LAC countries (from Maddison, 2003). It is not the aggregate growth for the region, because in that aggregate a few big countries determine the total value.

improve ties with the region, but Vice-President Nixon harbored serious misgivings about the whole idea.

The visit started in Uruguay, where there were some mild demonstrations. In Argentina, Nixon attended the presidential inauguration and was also able to address labor and university groups without major problems. The visit to Paraguay was relatively uneventful as well. However, there were angry mobs in Peru, both at the Universidad de San Marcos and at the hotel where the U.S. delegation stayed. On the other hand, in Ecuador and Colombia events were relatively pacific.

But all fury erupted in Caracas, where Nixon's presence provoked strong riots. Venezuela was the country that high U.S. officials, such as Henry Holland who was Assistant Secretary of State from 1954 to 1956, had praised as a model for the rest of the region: he considered Venezuela a "showcase of private enterprise," with a standard of living that exceeded other countries in the region (Rabe, 1988; p. 94). Yet, about five months before Nixon's arrival, Marcos Pérez Jiménez (former Venezuelan strong-man and recipient in 1954 of a medal from the Eisenhower Administration for his anti-communist efforts) had to flee the country forced by public demonstrations. He escaped accompanied by the hated chief of the secret police. Public sentiment against the United States was strong. Nixon's car was surrounded and pelted by rocks. The U.S. custody, fearing for the life of the Vice-President, had to rescue him. As Rabe (1988) notes "the ugly incident in Caracas was particularly unsettling for the administration: the Vice-President was nearly killed in the 'showcase' of U.S. policy in Latin America" (p. 102).

This trip opened a reassessment of U.S. policy towards the region. Back in Washington, Nixon suggested more support for democratic governments (as opposed to governments dominated by anti-communist autocrats) and funding for economic development. That was the approach that some high officials such as Under Secretary of State Douglas Dillon and unofficial advisors such as Milton Eisenhower had been advocating for some time without success.

In quick reaction to the incidents, on May 28 1958, President Kubitschek from Brazil sent a letter to President Eisenhower repudiating the attacks to the U.S. vice-president, which he attributed to a "factious minority." Kubitschek argued that "the ideal of Pan-American unity has suffered serious impairment." He reasoned that propaganda "directed toward presenting such supposed misunderstandings as actual incompatibility and even enmity between the free countries of the American community," would weaken "the cause of democracy, to the defense of which we are pledged." Therefore, the Brazilian president suggested that something had to be done "to restore composure to the continental unity." Kubitschek recognized that he did "have no definite and detailed plans to that effect," but he suggested "that the hour has come for us to undertake jointly a thorough review of the policy of mutual understanding on this Hemisphere and to conduct a comprehensive reappraisal of the proceedings already in motion for the furtherance of Pan-American ideals in all their aspects and implications" (Kubitschek's letter reproduced in Eisenhower, 1958a).

On June 5, Eisenhower answered in agreement with Kubitschek's argument regarding the need for "corrective measures" and the importance of holding consultations (Eisenhower, 1958a), and sent Secretary of State Dulles to Brazil on August 4. Dulles first tried, unsuccessfully, to convince Kubitschek that the main threat was Communism and that it had to be addressed basically as a police problem (Costa Couto, 1999). Kubitschek, however, maintained his view that it was needed to address both the security and the underdevelopment aspects of the problem. Finally, both signed a declaration, which reiterated "the conviction that the strengthening of the unity of the Americans requires...dynamic measures to defeat the problems of underdevelopment" and indicated "the belief that this principle -working for greater development, which is inseparable from the collective security of the hemisphere- should be upheld by the entire continent" (Costa Couto, 1999).

Other Latin American presidents were also involved in those exchanges, such as Argentina's Arturo Frondizi. He had also written to Eisenhower on June 4, a few days after Kubitschek, suggesting the need of Pan-American consultations on economic issues.[59]

---

[59] Frondizi, in a letter of June 4, noted that "many of the ills that afflict our world today have their origin in economic dislocations and maladjustments.... [N]ot a few of those ills stem from international factors...[T]he Argentine Government would be happy to support any initiative to reexamine and revise those economic policies, systems, or factors which affect the present state of affairs on the international level, or which hinder or delay the national unity of the American countries" (Frondizi's letter reproduced in Eisenhower, 1958b). On July 1, Eisenhower answered that he recognized and shared "the deep and common concern which arises from economic

On August 9, 1958 the Brazilian Government sent to the diplomatic missions of the OAS countries accredited in Brazil a document indicating that "the fight for democracy...has merged with the fight against underdevelopment." It suggested the creation of a committee in Washington to work on the foundations for the Pan-American Operation. The objectives proposed by Brazil for the Operation were: a) reaffirmation of principles of continental solidarity; b) underdevelopment as a common problem; c) adaptation of the Inter-American System to fight underdevelopment; d) technical assistance to improve productivity; e) measures to stabilize the markets for basic commodities; f) expansion of resources for international financial institutions, including the creation of a regional bank; g) reaffirmation of the importance of the private initiative to fight underdevelopment; and h) revision of fiscal and economic policies to ensure that they stimulate economic development (Broide, 1961).

Meanwhile, by 1958 problems in Middle East had expanded to Lebanon and other places. On July 15, 1958 President Eisenhower had ordered U.S. Marines into Lebanon at the request of President Camille. Trying to gain support for the U.S. approach to the conflict, which was being blocked by the Soviet veto at the Security Council, Eisenhower was scheduled to give a speech to the United Nations on August 13, 1958 about the Middle East situation. Eisenhower intended to announce a comprehensive plan for the Middle East that included the creation of a regional Arab development institution, "whose task would be to accelerate progress in such fields as industry, agriculture, water supply, health, and education" (Eisenhower, 1958c).

With that event rapidly approaching, Douglas Dillon, Milton Eisenhower and Roy Rubottom (then Assistant Secretary for Latin America at the State Department) wrote a memo to the U.S. president arguing that given the developments in the Americas it was untenable to announce another economic initiative outside Latin America while opposing a similar one for the region (Schlesinger, 1965). President Eisenhower agreed. A hastily arranged meeting of the OAS was

---

maladjustments and difficulties.... The desirability of joint consultation and discussions on economic factors and problems which are of mutual concern and impact is equally clear....I believe that in the present world situation it is more essential than ever for us to reaffirm the Pan-American tradition of cooperation and consultation. In the months to come there will be, I am sure, ample opportunities for an exchange of views among all the American Republics to this end" (Eisenhower, 1958b).

convened for August 12, where Douglas Dillon announced that the U.S. government was willing to proceed with the negotiations for the creation of a bank for Latin America.[60]

The next day President Eisenhower addressed the General Assembly of the United Nations, where he presented a framework for a peace plan which "would permit the peoples of the Near East to devote their energies wholeheartedly to the tasks of development and human progress in the widest sense." He also proposed consultations within the United Nations "to ascertain whether an agreement can be reached to establish an Arab development institution on a regional basis," which would "provide loans to the Arab States as well as the technical assistance required in the formulation of development projects." Eisenhower indicated that if the Arab States agreed to such institution and were prepared to support it with their own resources, then the United States would also participate. In Eisenhower's view, the institution should be governed by the Arab States themselves if it was going to succeed and should be organized in a way to attract international capital, both public and private.

Given the previous announcement of Douglas Dillon at the OAS, the president was also able to point out that the United States was working in partnership with the Organization of American States and "with our sister republics" in the Americas to strengthen the role of regional arrangements for economic development (Eisenhower, 1958c).

The principles outlined by the U.S. president in his speech to the United Nations were similar to what the Latin American countries had been suggesting for some time: they wanted to take responsibility and to have a key role in decision-making, knowing that it also meant that they had to allocate a substantial amount of the resources needed. This intention had been clearly demonstrated by the different previous proposals, particularly the last one from the Santiago meeting in 1955, in which two thirds of the resources were paid by Latin America. But, at the same time, Latin American countries did not think that a regional institution would be able to succeed without the participation of the United States. These ideas about burden sharing supported by

---

[60] It should be noted that the announcement happened several months before the overthrowing of Batista by Fidel Castro, which took place in January 1959. Although later in the decade U.S. policies for the region were very much influenced by the developments in Cuba, at least the decision to proceed with the creation of the IDB was unrelated to the political changes in the Caribbean island.

the countries in the region were in line with the Eisenhower Administration's views about the importance of self-help and the need to minimize the use of U.S. economic resources. Eisenhower was willing to let the developing countries of Latin America (and the Middle East) take a leadership role, to the extent that they were also prepared to assign the needed resources and take responsibility for the institution.[61] That was what Latin America had been waiting to hear for many decades.

d) The Creation of the Inter-American Development Bank

The work on the regional bank started at the Inter-American Economic and Social Council of the OAS with Resolution 30 (October 9, 1958) that convened the Committee of Twenty One "to negotiate and draft the instrument for the creation of an Inter-American financial institution." [62] The meeting was attended by President Eisenhower, who announced that "we will give top priority to problems in this hemisphere. Peace, security, and prosperity are indivisible for us all." According to press reports, "Secretary of State John Foster Dulles spared no energy to make [the meeting] a notable one. He led the talk over the entire broad range of problems that nag relations among the Americas. The work sessions produced a firm proposal for a hemisphere-development bank, an old Latin American dream agreed to by the United States for the first time in August." According to the press reports the meeting had generated one of the "warmest inter-American feelings in years" (Time Magazine, October 6, 1958).

The first working session of the Commission took place in Washington on January 12, 1959. The starting point of the work was a draft proposal presented by the U.S. delegates, but the debates led to modifications in some points (Broide, 1961). A topic debated was the

---

[61] The Arab institution never materialized.

[62] The number twenty one refers to the United States and the twenty Latin American countries that were members of the OAS at that time. The United States insisted on inviting only the member countries of the OAS to the Committee tasked with drafting the IDB agreement. This implied that observers from other international organizations were excluded. The reason for such insistence seems to have been the dislike that several members of the Eisenhower Administration had for ECLA and Prebisch. For instance, Dosman argued that "since the Bank would become the most important inter-American institution, U.S. officials wanted Prebisch as far away as possible from the key issues of policy, location and leadership" (Dosman, 2008, p. 341).

possibility of accepting deposits in the new bank. The 1890 International American Bank, the 1940 Inter-American Bank and the bank envisaged in the 1955 Santiago proposal, were all empowered to receive deposits from private agents and public institutions. This option, under pressure from private commercial banks, had disappeared when the World Bank was created and it was not included in the U.S. draft for the regional bank. Several Latin American delegates argued the need to maintain this funding option (that had been thoroughly analyzed and approved in Santiago), but their arguments did not prevail.

A second issue was related to the approval of loans in local currency. The proposal included the crucial innovation that the Bank could finance not only local costs, but to do that in local currency. To that effect the proposal for the new bank divided the capital in two types of shares: Class A, which funded ordinary loans in hard currency, and Class B, which financed loans that could be paid in local currency. These two types of capital had to be kept and managed completely separately from each other. The important distinction between market-based ("hard") and concessional ("soft") loans was incorporated in the Bank, which was created with two separate sources of funding: Ordinary Capital and the Fund for Special Operations (FSO). The latter would grant loans at very low interest rates, long repayment periods, and, under some circumstances, payable in local currencies.[63] Therefore, and different from the World Bank, the IDB had from the start a concessional window included in the Charter. In fact, that was one of the requests from Latin America to make the new regional bank different from the World Bank that the countries in the region considered to be too "commercial" and not interested in development issues.[64]

---

[63] According to the IDB Charter that was finally approved the payments in local currencies are subject to adjustments to maintain certain equivalence with the value originally agreed as measured in hard currency. This is called the "maintenance of value" obligation mandated in the Charter.

[64] Several years before the IDB's creation, John McCloy, then President of the World Bank, had argued in a meeting with the U.N. Economic and Employment Commission that he would not support the idea of a concessional window at the World Bank, which he referred to as a "bargain basement" (Sidney Dell, 1972, p. 21). In 1951, another World Bank president, Eugene Black reaffirmed in strong terms the opposition of the bank to soft loans in a meeting of the U.N. Economic and Social Council (Mason and Asher, 1973. p. 385). That position began to change when Senator Mike Monroney of Oklahoma, concerned about the accumulation of

Other debate within the Commission focused on the total capital base that the new regional institution needed to operate properly. The U.S. proposal suggested 700 million dollars for the Ordinary Capital, through the subscription of what were called Class A shares, and 150 million dollar for the concessional window, in Class B shares. Several countries in the region were pushing for a bigger bank: for instance, the Brazilian delegation wanted to reach about 5,000 million dollars, while Chile had floated the figure of 1,250 million dollars (Broide, 1961).[65] Finally, the total Ordinary Capital authorized for the Bank was 850 million dollars, which included both a paid-in component (400 million dollars payable in cash) and a committed, but not paid, callable capital (450 million dollars).[66] Another 150 million dollars were allocated to the concessional window, the Fund for Special Operations (FSO).[67]

About 60 percent of the Ordinary Capital and 33 percent of the resources for the FSO were subscribed by Latin American countries with the balance covered by the United States. Although there was some discussion in the Commission about allowing other countries to become members (for instance, Brazil suggested the inclusion of Canada and some European countries), the final decision restricted membership to

funds in local currencies as a result of the repayments of sales of U.S. agricultural surpluses to other countries, introduced in February 1958 a "sense of the Senate" resolution calling for the creation of an International Development Association within the World Bank Group, which could use those funds to make loans in local currencies. Eugene Black eventually revised his position and supported the Senate resolution, putting in motion a process that finally led to the creation of the concessional window of the World Bank in September 1960 (Mason and Asher, 1973). By then, the IDB had already been created with its concessional window.

[65] In March 2010 dollars the U.S. proposal amounted to 5,250 million dollars (Class A) and 1,125 million dollars (Class B). The Brazilian proposal amounted to 37,500 million dollars, while the Chilean proposal was about 9,375 million dollars.

[66] The callable capital acts as a guarantee. Originally, only the U.S. portion of that callable capital was counted by world financial markets when assessing the borrowing capacity of the IDB. Later, the callable capital utilized as a guarantee for IDB's borrowing in world financial markets extended also to the capital subscribed by other industrialized countries that joined the Bank. Those guarantees, along with IDB's preferred creditor status (i.e. the fact that borrowing members give preference to the Bank in the repayment of loans) and its strong capitalization, has allowed the IDB to borrow in world financial markets with a triple A rating and then pass those low interest rates to the borrowing member countries.

[67] The combined value of the Ordinary Capital and the FSO (1,000 million dollars) was equivalent to 7,500 million dollars of March 2010, considerably larger than the size of the bank discussed in Santiago in 1955.

countries that were members of the OAS. The value of the capital to be paid by Latin American countries was defined in proportion to their quotas at the IMF. After some discussions it was agreed that the payments to both funds could be done half in gold and U.S. dollars ("hard contributions") and half in local currencies ("soft contributions"). But, as already mentioned, the agreed Charter stipulated that the contributions in local currency should be maintained in value (to avoid that inflation in a country eroded the value of those payments).

During the debate in the Commission a detailed enumeration of the operations was discussed but then a simpler and more general description of functions was approved: a) to promote development through the investment of private and public capital, using its own capital, funds obtained through financial markets and other resources; b) to stimulate private investments and complement them when they were not available; c) to cooperate with member countries to orient development policies through the utilization of resources; d) to promote external trade; and e) to provide technical assistance for the preparation, financing, and execution of development programs and projects.

As in the financial institutions discussed so far, the authority rested on the Board of Governors (the Ministers or high officials of the member countries designated by their governments to exercise the voting power of their shares). The day-to-day operations were managed by the Board of Executive Directors (which were in turn designated by the Governors) and by the President of the Bank (who was elected by the Board of Governors and served under the direction of the Board of Executive Directors).

Other aspects incorporated into the Charter and also present in the Santiago proposal were the need to request the non-objection from the countries for the Bank to operate within any of them and the prohibition of requiring countries to buy from a single specific origin (instead of all members of the Bank) when sourcing goods and services for projects.

There were other important debates during the work of the Commission. One was the size and composition of the Board of Executives Directors, given that the original U.S. proposal would have left very little room for the representation of the smaller countries. The issue was solved by expanding the original number of Executive Directors from six to seven members.

Another discussion was the location of the headquarters of the Bank. A majority preferred to locate the institution in the United

States, but there were several Latin countries that argued that it was more appropriate to establish the headquarters of the Bank in Latin America (Venezuela in particular offered Caracas to host the new institution).[68] After the selection of the country, there was a second vote about the specific city within the United States and Washington was elected (nineteen delegations voted in favor but Cuba and Venezuela abstained) (Broide, 1961).

The name of the institution was approved during the meeting of March 25, 1959 of the Commission. The simpler name "Inter-American Development Bank," which had easy and direct translation to the four languages of the institution, was preferred to other options.[69]

Finally, on April 8, 1959 and after almost four months of deliberations, the Charter and all documents needed for the creation and operation of the Inter-American Development Bank were signed by all the delegates. The committee requested the OAS to keep the agreement open for signatures until December 1959.

A Preparatory Commission, with representatives from seven countries, was created to organize the first meeting of Governors and to draft the necessary documents to be considered in that meeting. The Preparatory Commission produced a series of proposals and plans concerning the different technical, legal, and administrative aspects related to the establishment of the IDB. That work proved to be crucial for the quick launching of the Bank as a functioning institution (Tomassini, 1997).

After the Executive branches completed their work, the proposal moved to the Legislatures of the countries involved. In the case of the United States, a formal proposal was sent to Congress to authorize the president to ratify the United States participation in the Bank and authorize the necessary initial funds (House Resolution 7072 and Senate Bill 1928, which were introduced as the Inter-American Development Bank Act). The letter of submission by President Eisenhower encouraged Congress to complete a quick passage of the proposed legislation. The Senate Committee of Foreign Relations took the lead on the bills and held hearings through June of 1959 (U.S. Senate, 1959).

---

[68] Bolivia, Costa Rica, Cuba, El Salvador, Panama and Venezuela voted to establish the bank in Latin America.

[69] The four languages are Spanish, English, Portuguese and French, which correspond to those of the founding member countries.

During the hearings in the U.S. Congress (June 3-23, 1959) Assistant Secretary of the Treasury, T. Graydon Upton, speaking on behalf of Secretary Anderson, testified before the Senate on the advantages of a development institution focused solely on Latin America. Under Secretary of State Douglas Dillon noted the political importance of the Bank, given the fact that poverty created a fertile ground for Communism. He also argued that the additionality of the new institution when compared with the World Bank, the IMF and the Export-Import Bank was that "the Bank is uniquely tailored to meet the needs of Latin America…[I]t is more than a financing institution. It is truly a development institution" (U.S. House of Representatives, 1959).

The developmental character of this institution was based on several new instruments and approaches the IDB had from the beginning and that later were also incorporated by the World Bank and other multilateral banks (see, for instance, Tomassini, 1997).

First, as already noted, the IDB was created with a concessional window, the FSO, that focused on certain types of program and projects, which could be paid back at lower interest, longer terms, and even in local currency. Without those concessional resources, low-income groups, less profitable social projects, and relatively less developed countries would not have had access to financial support. Combining loans at market rates using the Ordinary Capital with concessional operations through the FSO, the IDB was able to cover a larger spectrum of developmental challenges than existing financial institutions.

Second, from the beginning the IDB provided technical cooperation along with loans, something that the World Bank was unable to do at the time. Considering that one of the arguments against the creation of the regional bank had been that Latin America did not have enough viable projects, this instrument was crucial to support the technical and financial studies of the operations that were later financed. Technical cooperation helped to show that the projects existed, but what was needed was the "capacity building" required to develop them into "bankable" operations.

Third, the IDB was created with the possibility of financing not only individual projects, as it was the case of the World Bank, but also broader programs of economic development. This was important in the context of the Alliance for Progress (see below).

Fourth, the IDB was also allowed to finance operations with the private sector without governments' guarantees (Tomassini, 1997).

Besides those instruments and approaches, there were other clear differences with the World Bank. One was the regional character and the fact that from the beginning it focused on the integration of the Americas. This point was stressed by Felipe Herrera, the first president of the Bank, who was determined to give the institution a separate identity (Tomassini, 1997).

Finally, the most important characteristic was ownership and contribution of capital. In all existing financial institutions ownership of shares by the participating governments determined voting power. But different from the World Bank or the IMF, the IDB had a majority of shares paid by Latin American countries. In fact, although the IDB was derided as the "debtors' bank" by its critics (Tomassini, 1997), the Senate Foreign Affairs Committee viewed with approval the fact that the developing countries in the region would make significant financial contributions to the capital of the institution. This burden sharing, apart from being what Latin American countries wanted, was in line with the principles set out by President Eisenhower and addressed the concerns of the fiscally conscious legislators (and the U.S. Treasury Department), that did not want open-ended financial commitments funded only by the United States. The legislators also concurred with the importance of providing funding and technical assistance at a regional level, as opposed to the global scope of the Bretton Woods institutions.

As in previous debates about a regional financial institution, some of the persons that testified during the hearings criticized the potentially overlapping functions with existing institutions and stressed the importance to prioritize private, and not public, funding for development. But this time those criticisms were ignored.

The bill was approved by the House with 230 votes in support and 87 votes against. The Senate adopted the House bill without amendments. At the signing ceremony of the legislation, President Eisenhower characterized the IDB as the "most significant step in the history of our economic relations with our Latin American neighbors" (Trussell, 1959).

The ratification of the Agreement at the OAS started on October 14, 1959, with the signatures of Argentina and the United States. The next country to sign the ratification was Haiti on October 27. Then at different dates during November and December the rest of the founding members (Venezuela, Guatemala, Paraguay, Dominican Republic, Chile, Colombia, Ecuador, El Salvador, Honduras, Nicaragua, Panama, Bolivia,

Brazil, Costa Rica, Mexico, and Peru) ratified the agreement. Uruguay did it in February 1960, while Cuba never did.

The first meeting of Governors took place in San Salvador, El Salvador on February 3-16, 1960.[70] There, Felipe Herrera, who had been an active participant in the several meetings and consultations related to the creation of the Bank during the 1950s, was elected as the first president of the Inter-American Development Bank. [71]

e) The Bogotá Act, the Alliance for Progress, and the Launching of the Bank

The reassessment of the Latin American policy within the Eisenhower Administration in 1958 and 1959 that led to the creation of the IDB, while inserted in the Cold War competition with the Soviet Union, was, as argued before, not initially related to the developments in Cuba. However, by early 1960 the events in the Caribbean country had sharpened the concerns in the Eisenhower Administration about the potential appeal of Communism in Latin America. A consequence was that President Eisenhower instituted the National Advisory Committee on Inter-American Affairs in November 1959 and the next year created the position of Undersecretary of State for Inter-American Affairs to show the interest of his Administration in the region (Rabe, 1988).

In February 1960 President Eisenhower visited Argentina, Brazil, Chile, and Uruguay, where, different from Nixon's trip less than two years before, he was well received. In his visit, Eisenhower heard repeatedly from his interlocutors that the problem was not Castro but poverty and underdevelopment. The Eisenhower Administration concluded that an anti-communist policy was not enough and that the

---

[70] According to Dosman (2008) the distrust of Prebisch by the U.S. government was again reflected in the fact that Douglas Dillon and Thomas Mann, both high U.S. officials in inter-American affairs, made sure that he was not invited to the first Governors meeting in San Salvador. Although Dosman does not elaborate, the fact that the first president of the IDB was going to be elected at that meeting may explain why Prebisch was not invited.

[71] Felipe Herrera had participated at the Quitandinha meeting of 1954, and he had also been a member of the Committee of Experts that worked in Santiago, Chile, in 1955. In 1958, while he was in Washington D.C. as representative of his country at the IMF, he was involved in discussions on the drafting of the bylaws of the IDB. Finally, Herrera had an important role in the Preparatory Commission that drafted the different technical, legal and administrative proposals that, as mentioned before, were very important for the quick start up of the Bank (Tomassini, 1997).

political, economic and social structures of Latin America also needed reform (Rabe, 1988, p. 133). To gain support for its Cuban policy, the U.S. government came to believe that what was needed was "a dramatic, U.S. backed, democratic development program" (Rabe, 1988, p.137). An OAS conference was called to discuss development and social issues later in the year at Bogota, Colombia.

In July 1960, in a news conference at Newport, Rhode Island, while talking about his trip to Latin America, President Eisenhower noted that "each period in history brings its call for supreme human effort...At times in the past it took the form of war. Today it takes the form of social evolution or revolution. The United States will not, cannot stand aloof. We must help find constructive means for the under-privileged masses of mankind to work their way toward a better life. Indeed, so far as this Hemisphere is concerned, every American nation must cooperate in this mighty endeavor" (Eisenhower, 1960).

He also mentioned the preparatory work being done for the Bogota meeting, where "an equally important component of our hemispheric future --the problem of social reform and economic growth," was going to be considered, "within a joint hemispheric concept known as Operation Pan-America --a concept initially suggested by President Kubitschek of Brazil." Then Eisenhower announced that he was seeking authority from Congress "for such additional public funds as we may deem appropriate to assist free men and neighbors in Latin America in cooperative efforts to develop their nations and achieve better lives" (Eisenhower, 1960). Those funds, announced to be up to 500 million dollars (about 3,700 million dollars in March 2010 currency), became the Social Progress Trust Fund (SPTF) for health, education, housing, and land reform projects, which was later assigned to the IDB for its administration.[72]

The Bogotá Conference in September, 1960, few weeks before the elections that would bring back the Democrats to the White House,

---

[72] It is interesting to note that, in a recurrent theme in development debates, "developmentalist" Presidents in Latin America, such as Kubistchek and Frondizi, were not that enthusiastic about the social investments envisaged by the Social Progress Trust Fund, which they considered only as a small palliative for deeper social and economic problems. They believed that what was needed was a full-fledged development program, with a strong focus on industrialization (see for instance Schlesinger, 1965, p. 176 on Frondizi's misgivings; p. 191 on lukewarm feelings in Latin America related to the SPTF approach).

produced the "Acta de Bogotá," a stirring call for economic and social reforms that anticipated many aspects of the Alliance for Progress.

A few months after that, John Kennedy, in his inaugural presidential address promised to "our sister republics south of our border," a "special pledge -- to convert our good words into good deeds in a new alliance for progress --to assist free men and free governments in casting off the chains of poverty" (Kennedy, 1961). Weeks later in March, 1961, President Kennedy announced the largest U.S. aid program toward the developing world up to that point: the Alliance for Progress, a ten-point, ten-year economic and social development plan for Latin America, in which the United States pledged to contribute half of the 20,000 million dollars announced for the program (about 140,000 million dollars in March 2010 currency). This was the amount that, according to estimates of specialists, the region required to finance sustained economic growth, fund social reforms to help the poorest Latin Americans, promote democracy, and strengthen ties in the Americas.

The program also called for substantial reform of Latin American structures and institutions: the Declaration to the Peoples of America and the Charter of the Alliance for Progress, signed both in August 1961 in Punta del Este, Uruguay, listed a set of ambitious objectives. They included: the improvement and strengthening of democratic institutions; acceleration of economic and social development; urban and rural housing programs; programs of agrarian reform; fair wages and satisfactory working conditions for all workers; elimination of illiteracy and increase in the number of schools for secondary and higher education; expansion of programs of health and sanitation; reform of tax laws, "demanding more from those who have most;" monetary and fiscal policies that protected purchasing power; stimulus to private enterprise; solution to the problems created by excessive price fluctuations in basic commodity exports; and acceleration of economic integration in Latin America (Declaration of Punta del Este, 1961; Charter of Punta del Este, 1961).

As Dosman (2008) notes the Alliance for Progress was "a version of 'progressive capitalism' based in a spirit of mutual interest and respect, in which Latin ideas were once again welcomed...The U.S. delegation at Punta del Este came to incorporate virtually the entire ECLA program in the Charter, including many ideas that Washington had fought with very strong language since its creation" (p. 360-362).[73]

Taking place almost immediately after the inspiring March announcement by President Kennedy, the Bay of Pigs invasion in April 1961 was an early indicator of the broader geopolitical difficulties that the Alliance would face. But there were also problems within Latin American countries themselves, where economic elites resisted the changes envisaged in the Declaration and Charter of Punta del Este. Democracy was also weakened by sixteen military coups in the first eight years of the Alliance. U.S. commitment was shifting, moving from a vision of democratic and inclusive development in 1961-1963 to one with an increasing concern about security issues.

But the decisions of the Eisenhower Administration in the context of the Bogotá Act, later continued and enlarged in the expansive development program of the Alliance for Progress, were crucial for the strong starting of the IDB: in June 1961 the Social Progress Trust Fund, originally proposed by President Eisenhower but then implemented under the Kennedy Administration, was created with almost 400 million dollars (about 2,800 million dollars in March 2010 terms), and, as mentioned, the IDB was designated as its administrator. Therefore for several years at the beginning of the Bank, the institution had two facilities that provided loans on concessional terms: the FSO as defined in the Charter and the Social Progress Trust Fund.

Both funds, which received additional funding during the first years of the Alliance for Progress, were fundamental for the initial operations of the IDB and its quick establishment as a key financial entity for the region. Without the concessional windows the IDB would have only had the resources of the Ordinary Capital, which allowed the Bank to borrow in world markets at market rates, and then to relend with a spread over those rates, as the World Bank did. But in the early 1960s, when the IDB was just starting, the World Bank was already an established institution with a triple A rating, which allowed it to borrow cheaper in world markets and, therefore, could offer more favorable rates to Latin

---

[73] Dosman (2008) also reports that in April 1961 Prebisch, who had been "civilly tolerated" by the Eisenhower administration but which had always "kept him at arm's length," was invited by the new Democrat Administration to the White House to meet with the top Kennedy people ahead of the Punta del Este meeting. Regarding that meeting Prebisch is quoted as saying that "I've headed ECLA for over a decade now and this is a wonderful experience for me because for the first time a high-level U.S. delegate has talked to me as an equal" (Dosman, 2008, p.359).

American borrowers than the IDB. However, the IDB was able to compensate its higher funding costs by offering to its borrowers a mix of loans at commercial rates from the Ordinary Capital and loans on soft terms from the two concessional windows. Moreover, as already mentioned, the two concessional funds allowed the IDB to venture into projects with longer-term and more indirect payoffs, which the commercial terms of the Ordinary Capital would not have been able to accommodate. It can be then argued that the bipartisan support in the United States from the Eisenhower and Kennedy Administrations to finance the concessional windows of the IDB was crucial for the take off of this institution during the 1960s. Over time, the financing of the FSO also began to show a stronger component of regional solidarity, with borrowing member countries contributing growing percentages to the concessional windows and more advanced borrowing countries accepting to receive less and less of those resources (see next chapter).

The IDB started its operations on October 1, 1960 with almost 190 employees at Bank headquarters in Washington, D.C. That same year, the Bank approved the first technical assistance operation: 61,500 dollars to support the institutional strengthening of the mining sector in Bolivia. The following year there were also pioneering technical assistance operations for fourteen countries. Also, in 1961 the IDB approved the first loan from Ordinary Capital for 3.9 million dollars to finance water and sanitation installations in Arequipa, Peru. It was the type of socially-oriented projects that other institutions did not finance at that time, although they would do it later when the positive impacts of these investments were better appreciated.[74] Other similar loans followed that year for Brazil, Chile, Colombia, El Salvador, Uruguay, and Venezuela. The same year, the first FSO project was approved: 10 million dollars for a global credit program (agriculture, electrical energy, and industry) in Bolivia. These operations inaugurated a new way of lending to smaller private firms in the region: the IDB lent a global amount to a domestic financial institution, which would then conduct the individual credit assessment and on-lend directly to small borrowers. Also, innovating with respect to other institutions, the Bank appointed a representative in Bolivia, which

---

[74] Enrique Iglesias tells the following anecdote: Eugene Black, then President of the World Bank, after learning about those water operations, called Felipe Herrera and told him: "Felipe, you must have a very liquid institution" (Iglesias, 2005).

led eventually to the system of country offices in each one of the borrowing member countries.[75]

Latin American countries had attained the long-awaited goal: a regional financial institution with significant resources in which they had a strong voice in decision-making and management. In fact, for the first time, developing countries had a majority position through ownership of shares backed with their own capital. Notwithstanding the misgivings about the possible performance of an institution "managed by debtors," the IDB since Felipe Herrera operated prudently as a cooperative of owners, achieving and maintaining a strong credit rating while supporting the economic and social development of the region.[76] The next decades would show how important that aspiration and that vision were to become.

Now that the IDB is in the process of implementation of a new increase of capital (the Ninth since its creation), the Bank has to renew itself for the challenges of the decades to come. To do that it is important to remember the historical developments that led to its creation in the first place. The next concluding chapter is an attempt to such retrospective-prospective exercise.[77]

---

[75] Currently, in addition to the headquarters in Washington D.C., there are twenty-six offices in LAC countries and two additional offices, one for Europe (in France) and another for Asia (in Japan).

[76] Nancy Birdsall (a former Vice-president of the IDB) noted in an article that discussed governance in international financial institutions, that "there is at least some evidence that [the] effectiveness [of international institutions] is reduced directly for lack of developing country influence, and indirectly because that dearth of influence reduces their legitimacy. The evidence, based loosely on the effects of greater influence of borrowers in the Inter-American Development Bank, is not only that the developing countries need the multilateral institutions, but that institutions can benefit from their greater influence" (Birdsall, 2003).

[77] Before 2010 there have been eight capital increases: the First in 1964; the Second in 1968; the Third in 1970; the Fourth in 1976; the Fifth in 1980; the Sixth in 1983; the Seventh in 1990; and the Eight in 1994. At the time this book is being written, the Ninth replenishment has been already negotiated and is in the process of being ratified by the legislatures of the individual countries.

Understanding the Past, Thinking about the Future

The history of the creation of the Inter-American Development Bank illustrates some enduring features of the relations between Latin America and the United States. Such features have also been present in different degrees during the five decades since the creation of the Bank and, therefore, they may have implications for the future operations of the institution. In this concluding chapter we try to highlight four broad topics related to a) international politics in the region; b) economic development; c) international structures of governance and resources; and d) some reflections on dialogue and building consensuses at the IDB.

The next sections are organized in two parts: first, some historical perspective is provided for each of those four general topics, using both the narrative of the previous chapters leading to the creation of the IDB and also some briefs references to events *after* the institution was established; second, some reflections for the future are presented.

a) International Politics and Democracy

Historical Perspectives

A well-known fact of hemispheric relations is the U.S. quest to limit external influences in the Americas, which has had three different, but in many cases interrelated, components: security (military presence), economic (trade and financial links), and political (governance structure and ideology). The institutional narrative of the previous chapters highlights the importance and the changing role of those components in the history of the creation of the IDB.

Once the United States completed the military expansion and emerged united from the Civil War, U.S. interests in Latin America shifted to economic matters in the last decades of the nineteenth century, shaping the interaction with the European powers present in the region during that period. Therefore, the proposal of the International American

Bank in 1889/90 was part of a larger *economic* plan to compete and, eventually, to try to displace the United Kingdom and other European countries in the expanding Latin American markets.

During the 1930s, the Roosevelt Administration grew increasingly alarmed about the possibility of another world war and the advance of Nazism and Fascism in the Americas. A central concern was the possibility that the substantial reservoir of raw materials in Latin America, which were important to sustain the war effort, could fall in the hands of the Axis Powers. Therefore, the 1940 Inter-American Bank was predicated on the need to keep those war enemies out of the region. Different from the mainly economic considerations for the creation of the 1890 Bank, the reasons for establishing a regional bank in 1940 were mostly based on *military and security* considerations.

Finally, the U.S. acceptance of the creation of the IDB in 1959 was firmly inscribed in a desire to limit Soviet influence in the Americas as part of the Cold War. Along with the security and military component there were also strong *political and ideological* considerations, influenced in part by the mid-1950s change in strategy by the Soviet Union that started to emphasize the use of economic and technical cooperation to expand its influence in the developing regions. At the same time, the deterioration of Latin American economic and social conditions in the late 1950s led to an increasing realization in the United States that poverty and social unrest could facilitate the spread of Soviet influence. The reevaluation of the U.S. policy towards Latin America by the Eisenhower Administration provided the general framework for the events that led to the creation of the IDB.

The Cuban revolution had not yet happened in 1958 when that reevaluation took place, and therefore the creation of the IDB cannot be attributed to developments in that country. But the events in Cuba were the main background for the deepening of the developmental and social perspectives both in the Act of Bogotá in 1960, signed by the outgoing Eisenhower Administration, and also in the intellectual successor to that Act, the 1961 Alliance for Progress, which offered a strong platform for the consolidation of the IDB after its creation.

With the IDB already firmly established, a period not discussed in the previous chapters, the Cold War conflict with Communism and the Soviet Union was a factor behind the resignations of the first and second presidents of the IDB. The strong opposition of the Nixon Administration to the election of Salvador Allende as president of Chile in September

1970 presaged growing conflicts between both countries. Trying to separate the IDB from the coming confrontation, Felipe Herrera, who was Allende's friend and shared the same political affiliation, resigned in October 1970 shortly after the Chilean presidential election.[78]

Several years later Antonio Ortiz Mena's resignation was in part linked to the divisions between several Latin American countries and the Reagan Administration over Nicaragua and the political situation in Central America during the 1980s. The Sandinistas had ousted Somoza in 1979 and received some support from the Carter Administration. However, U.S. policies towards the country changed with the Reagan Administration in 1981. The new U.S. government began to oppose loans from the IDB and the World Bank to Nicaragua. During the mid 1980s there were strong clashes within the IDB involving U.S. and LAC representatives, as well as Bank's management, about the proper treatment of the Nicaraguan loans by the Board of Executive Directors. A particular governance issue was the fact that loans funded with the Ordinary Capital can be approved by a simple majority of the shares and Latin American countries, as a whole, have held that majority since the creation of the Bank.[79] Therefore, the Reagan Administration wanted to have the option of postponing for an extended period the treatment by the Board of OC loans. When the IDB was running out of resources in the late 1980s, these governance issues were hotly debated and were part of the disagreements that provided the context for Ortiz Mena's resignation in December 1987.

These developments were in line with Krasner's (1981) observation that, during the Cold War period, U.S. governments considered IDB's most important function the promotion of a pattern of development that would frustrate what was perceived as Soviet expansion in the region.

---

[78] Some articles in influential U.S. newspapers started direct attacks against Felipe Herrera using the political affiliation of the president of the IDB (see, for instance, two articles by Jack Anderson in the Washington Post: "Herrera Devised Rare Bank Services," February 13, 1970; and "Latin Bank Chief's Loans Scrutinized," May 27, 1970).

[79] While the IDB Charter establishes that decisions related to operations funded by the Ordinary Capital require a simple majority, loans financed by the Fund of Special Operations need a special majority (three fourth of the voting power by shares; Article IV, Section 9 b). Since the establishment of the Bank the United States has had enough voting power to block any FSO project simply by abstaining (currently the United States has 30 percent of the shares).

Current and Future Challenges

Moving to the present, and with the disappearance of the Soviet Union, a question may be whether there is any type of international interference that the United States may want to keep outside the region, and, if so, what would the expected role of the IDB be in that regard. Concerns about external interferences may not be now from specific countries, considering that the United States encouraged in the 1970s and 1980s the participation of European countries and Japan in the IDB, and in the 2000s, supported as well the membership of Korea and China in the Bank.

Now the extraneous and negative factors whose influence must be sharply reduced and/or kept out of the region are basically transnational problems, such as drug-trafficking, organized crime, money laundering, and terrorism. Updating Krasner's point, the issue would now be the design of broad-based and socially inclusive development strategies that help the region resist those transnational scourges. It is difficult to see any divergence among IDB's member countries about the importance of such objective. The Bank may need to expand its research and strengthen its programs focusing on these problems as a way to better help the countries in the region.

A separate topic, related to the political component of U.S. regional aims, has been the interest of the United States since Thomas Jefferson in the "sister republics" of the South because of the assumed commonality in governance approaches. Blocking external powers in the Americas included the need to keep monarchical, nazi-fascist, and communist forms of government out of the region. Authoritarian and non-democratic military governments were, however, tolerated and, at times, supported by the some U.S. Administrations because those governments were considered to provide some resemblance of order and stability and kept other forms of totalitarian rule out of the region. This was perceived as double standard by many in Latin America during the 1960s and 1970s, when more than 70 percent of the countries in the region were classified as non democratic (see Polity IV, 2009). However, there were also cases in which the U.S. Congress passed legislation that mandated U.S. representatives at the IDB and other multilateral organizations to vote against loans for some military governments in the region (such as the case of the Pinochet government in Chile).

The general issue of democracy and the type of government in borrowing member countries has been a matter of debate within the IDB. The Bank's Charter stipulates that lending decisions must be based on economic criteria "impartially weighed," and it further states that "the Bank, its officers and employees shall not interfere in the political affairs of any member, nor shall they be influenced in their decisions by the political character of the member or members concerned" (Article VIII, Section 5 (f)). Therefore the IDB operated for many years under the criterion that the institution worked for the *people* of the region, whatever the form of the *government* that happened to hold the voting shares at the IDB at that time (therefore, it sufficed to look at the social and economic impacts of the projects as determined in Article I of the Charter).

This approach was basically followed during the 1960s and 1970s even though the proper link between governments and the people they should represent was broken during the many painful episodes of non-democratic governments in the region. Fortunately, since the mid-1980s, the sustained democratic advances in Latin America and the Caribbean have reinstated the legitimate links between people and governments. The IDB continues to perform its functions through governments that hold, temporarily, the fiduciary responsibility for the shares of the Bank on behalf of that people; and, since the return of democracy to the region, those governments have been entrusted by voters with the authority and responsibility associated to those shares.

The advance of democracy in the region strengthened the legitimacy of the institution and opened new areas of work. Under the leadership of Enrique Iglesias, IDB's third and longest-serving president, the Bank assumed a strongly supportive role in the process of consolidating democratic institutions in the region. New topics related to improved governance, transparency, and democratic participation, were incorporated as areas eligible for lending. Also, and always in coordination with the Organization of American States, the IDB has applied a "democratic clause" to interrupt lending in cases when a democratic government was toppled by a coup d'état and the country was suspended as member of the OAS.[80]

---

[80] The legal basis for that decision is that Article II Section 1 of the Charter indicates that countries in the region must be members of the OAS to also belong to the IDB. This requisite does not apply to extra-regional members.

It must be recognized that the combination of a Bank with a majority participation of developing countries and borrowing member countries with democratic governments sets the IDB apart from other multilateral financial organizations. This should be remembered when requests for greater "civil society" participation are applied mechanically across institutions without recognizing the diversity of institutional frameworks.

While in other developing regions a larger percentage of countries is still classified as non democratic (see Polity IV, 2009), the wave of democratization has reached deeper in the societal structures of most countries in Latin America and the Caribbean. Although the region suffered painful economic crises in the 1990s and early 2000s, countries emerged from those difficult events through broadly democratic means. Also, the participation and enfranchisement of groups and peoples previously at the margins of the democratic process, such as the case of indigenous populations, have expanded significantly. Inevitably, these changes have led to democratic structures and processes that are still evolving, with important advances but also frailties and weaknesses, and which will require time to decant into more stable democracies.

The global crisis initiated in the second half of 2007, now with Luis Alberto Moreno as fourth president of the IDB, has been testing again the strength of the institutional advances in the region. As of this writing (end of 2010), the region appears to go through an unequal recovery from the global crisis, with Mexico, Central America and the Caribbean still affected by the deep economic recession in the United States, while South America, buoyed by low interest rates, capital inflows, and strong commodity prices, is having a stronger economic performance. In that context, several countries in the region have managed, since the start of the crisis, to stage democratic presidential and legislative elections in which power changed hands peacefully. Yet there have been, and still are, challenges to democracy in the region, affected not only by the transnational scourges mentioned above, but also by the perennial problems of poverty and inequality.

All in all, the Bank must continue to support the strengthening of democracies in the region, letting the social process of self-discovery run its course, avoiding impatience and hasty judgments. The best approach for the Bank to support democracy and reduce the influence of transnational problems continues to be based on the need to promote equitable economic development with socially inclusive and integrated societies that function under democratic rule.

In any case, the example of a developing region managing its development process through democratic means (even admitting the occasional lapses) should be appreciated as a contribution to global stability and civilized behavior.

b) Economic Issues: Finances and Trade

Historical Perspectives: Financial Issues

A second theme that is evident from the history of the creation of the IDB is the influence of global economic conditions on the interaction between Latin America and the United States and, therefore, in the ups and downs of the idea of a regional bank. The negotiations for the first International American Bank of 1890, which was a private sector institution, coincided with a time of highly mobile capital and labor, and of mounting debts in Latin America. The vulnerability of the export-driven economies to changes in commodity prices tied those countries to volatile capital flows and cycles of expansion and decline in the foreign demand for their products. Booms and busts were associated with the growth cycle in the region's main trading partners –basically Great Britain in the nineteenth century and the United States in the twentieth century. Those cycles provided the background for Latin America's interest in a regional bank. With the value of exports correlated to changes in the money supply and with pro-cyclical fiscal policies aggravating public deficits, Latin American governments actively sought a bank when the commodity and financial conditions were unfavorable, but the intensity of interest diminished when economic conditions improved.

From the point of view of the United States, economic interests clearly shaped the proposal of the 1890 International American Bank. Private sector financiers and merchants hoped to expand into Latin American markets but lacked the financial instruments given the legal limitations to operate internationally and to establish branches abroad faced by the U.S. banks. The Latin countries, while not without some doubts, were basically receptive to the idea of a regional bank, perhaps also influenced by the reverberations of the Baring Bank crisis among European investors.

After the failure to approve the creation of the International American Bank, the discussion about regional financial institutions began to shift towards the issue of the stability of currencies and exchange rates, in line with the problems experienced by the gold standard before and during World War I. The enactment of legislation creating the Federal Reserve in 1913, which included regulations that allowed U.S. banks to conduct business abroad, eliminated the problem that the 1890 International American Bank was supposed to solve. Therefore, while during the late nineteenth and early twentieth centuries the United States and Latin America sought a banking institution to finance and expand trade, around the time of the World War I the attention shifted to the stabilization of exchange rates to facilitate regional commerce. The mid-1910s proposal of the Gold Clearance Fund Convention and the idea of extending the work of the Federal Reserve to all the Americas, tried to address those new challenges. These extremely ambitious ideas were mostly set aside once the gold standard was restored following World War I. After that war the United States became a net international creditor and trade within the Americas expanded.

The idea of a stabilization fund for exchanges rates re-emerged from time to time, mostly during periods of exchange-rate volatility and as a result of "beggar-thy-neighbor" devaluations during the 1930s. The idea of an international mechanism to stabilize exchange rates finally materialized with the creation of the International Monetary Fund. But before that the world had to first experience the multiple economic, financial, and commercial challenges generated by the Great Depression in the 1930s, and World War II.

With war tensions increasing in Europe, the 1940 Inter-American Bank was conceived as an all-encompassing financial institution, with functions of a commercial, investment, and Central Bank, and with a strong participation from the public sector. It was supposed to address not only the issue of exchange rate volatility and trade finance, but also other problems linked to longer term investments in the region.

The idea of such a powerful bank proved to be too menacing for the U.S. private banks and they found allies in the U.S. Congress that successfully blocked its legislative approval. Eventually, the ideas behind the 1940 Bank were implemented half a decade later with the creation of the World Bank and the IMF, although this happened in a scaled-down and partitioned version of the original institution.

The global economic slump after the Korean War contributed to the social unrest in Latin America and the Caribbean that eventually led to the creation of the IDB: the United States suffered a recession in 1954 after the war ended in 1953 and had three years of weak or negative growth in 1956, 1957, and 1958, which affected most Latin American countries.

With the IDB already created, the period of strong world and regional growth during the 1960s, coupled with the excitement of the joint U.S.-LAC program centered on the Alliance for Progress, provided strong support for the consolidation and expansion of the Bank, under the leadership of Felipe Herrera. The brand of "progressive capitalism" embedded in the Declaration and Charter of Punta del Este of 1961, which reflected much of ECLA's program under Prebisch, called for industrialization, agrarian reform, equitable taxes, expanded education, social investments, and regional integration. The IDB helped with financing and technical assistance on many fronts. However, some of the reforms generated resistance in dominant groups in the region. A manifestation of the existing problems was the fact that within the first eight years of the Alliance there were sixteen military coups in the region. Also the hardening of a geopolitical setting defined by the Cold War and the challenges of the Cuban Revolution were changing the context for the Bank, and eventually led to Felipe Herrera's resignation as its first President.

During the 1970s, the IDB, guided by Antonio Ortiz Mena as its second president, assisted the region during a succession of shocks, including the food and oil price crises. The Bank was again present during the debt problems of the 1980s that led to the so-called "lost decade" in Latin America. Ortiz Mena is justly remembered as the president who made the IDB a truly international organization, with the admission to membership of Canada, several European countries, and Japan. But it is as important to recognize his leadership as he piloted the Bank through those difficult economic times in which the institution continued to grow and innovate.

Particularly during the "debt crisis" fresh economic ideas were needed and the IDB experimented with new approaches. The IDB pioneered global loans to help with balance-of-payment problems but these operations were maintained within the context of the developmental policies followed so far in the region. The Reagan Administration, however, insisted on the need of economic policy changes in the region. Those changes were later embedded in the loans called of "structural adjustment," which were started by the World Bank. Global loans for budget and balance-of payment support had not been viewed favorably by many Latin American officials and analysts during the discussions of the 1940 Bank and in the 1955 Santiago meeting (see for instance Villaseñor 1941 and 1948). Moreover, the policy conditionality that was being attached to those operations was regarded with great distrust by those believing in the "developmentalist" credo that imbued the economic policies of many Latin American countries. These differences in approaches to economic policies, along with the Cold War events in Central America, affected the Bank in the late 1980s and provided the background for the resignation of Ortiz Mena.

The acceleration of the economy in the 1990s ushered a new period of expansion for the IDB. The Bank, after the Seventh and Eighth capital increases, approved in 1990 and 1994 under the leadership of Enrique Iglesias, became the largest source of development loans in Latin America, overtaking the World Bank in the region.

Following the economic crises of the late 1990s and early 2000s, world financial markets entered a period of excess liquidity. This prompted a debate about the potential marginalization of multilateral financial institutions and the need for a very precise specialization on issues such as fighting poverty and the generation of public goods that markets could not provide. Another avenue of further work for the Bank was to refocus its work from national governments to sub-national entities.

This debate ended after the significant increase in the public sector demand for loans from the IDB and other international financial institutions that followed the global financial crisis, started in the second half of 2007. Urged by their member countries, those financial institutions expanded lending significantly during the crisis. As a result of that expansion they became constrained for further lending and, therefore, the IDB and other financial institutions required a replenishment of capital.[81]

---

[81] For instance, the Eighth Capital increase of the IDB expanded its capital base and allowed the Bank to lend about 6,000/7,000 million dollars per year, on a sustained basis. Because of the increased demand linked to the crisis, the IDB had to step up its operations: approvals went up to about 11,000 million dollars in 2008 and 15,900 million dollars in 2009. In 2010 the level of approvals has been 12,900 million dollars, in between the 2008 and 2009 levels. Without the current capital increase (the Ninth), Bank's lending would have to decline below the pre-crisis average.

Now, the strains in global financial markets and the unlikely prospects for (and undesirability of) a return to the excesses of liquidity and leverage that created the current crisis, define a framework that may require an increased role for multinational financial institutions, such as the IDB (see below).

So far we have discussed the changing global financial conditions and their impacts, first, on the idea of a regional financial institutions, and, second, once the IDB was created, on its functioning. However, the discussion of economic aspects would be incomplete without a special reference to trade and integration issues, both in the creation of the Bank and in its subsequent operations.

Historical Perspectives: Trade and Integration Issues

Since the Congress of Panama organized by Simón Bolivar in 1826, regional commerce and navigation, as well as other aspects of economic integration, were discussed at different inter-American meetings (see Maisch, 2004). The early discussions about a regional bank or about funds to stabilize exchange rates were linked to the desire of expanding trade in the Americas. The 1940 Inter-American Bank also included among its objectives the support to trade expansion and integration in the region.

Therefore, it is not surprising that when the IDB was finally created, the mandate related to integration was clear in its Charter: the first paragraph states that "the purpose of the Bank shall be to contribute to the acceleration of the process of economic and social development of the regional developing member countries, individually and *collectively (emphasis added by the authors)*" (Article I, Section 1). Felipe Herrera, who always called the IDB the "integration bank," took a holistic view to the mandate of attaining development "collectively." He believed that "the nation of Latin America is not a fictional entity. It is at the root of our modern states and persists as a vital force and a profound reality...Latin America is not a group of nations: it is one great, fragmented nation" (quoted in Tomasini, 1997, p. 99-100).

The Alliance for Progress, which included a specific commitment on regional economic integration in the Declaration and Charter of Punta del Este, gave further impulse to the process. Although the conceptual and technical foundations were provided mainly by the work of Raúl Prebisch and ECLAC, the IDB supported in 1960 the implementation of regional and sub-regional integration agreements, such as the Montevideo Treaty that established the Latin American Free Trade Association (ALALC), and the Managua Treaty, which created the Central American Common Market. The same happened later with the CARICOM in the English-speaking Caribbean countries; with the Cartagena Treaty that created the Andean Pact; and with sub-regional banks such as the Central American Bank of Economic Integration (CABEI), the Caribbean Development Bank, and the Corporación Andina de Fomento (CAF) (see Bouzas and Knaack, 2009).

Additionally, the IDB also created the Pre-investment Fund for Latin American Integration to finance regional feasibility studies and invested in the first regional projects related to roads, telecommunications, and electricity. In 1965, with strong support from the Illia Administration in Argentina, the Bank established the Institute for Latin American Integration (INTAL) in Buenos Aires, with the objective of functioning as "a center for research, advisory assistance, higher education, and the exchange and dissemination of integration experiences in Latin America" (Tomassini, 1997, p.105).[82]

The economic shocks of the mid and late 1970s and the debt crisis of the 1980s not only affected economic and financial conditions in the region but also slowed down the process of regional integration (Bouzas and Knaack, 2009). But since the late 1980s, with the return to democracy, there was also renewed interest in sub-regional trade agreements, including some new initiatives, such as MERCOSUR, conformed initially by Argentina, Brazil, Paraguay and Uruguay. The IDB was deeply involved in all those trade and integration initiatives, both at the sub-regional and regional levels (see Bouzas and Knaack, 2009).

Also, during the 1990s, with more favorable economic and political conditions in the region, the Administration of George H.W. Bush and governments in Latin America and the Caribbean opened a new period of convergence and cooperation. In June 1990, the Enterprise for the Americas Initiative (EAI) was unveiled with the purpose of fostering hemispheric trade integration, market-oriented economic policies, and democratic governance.[83] The negotiations for the Free Trade Agreement of the Americas (FTAA), and other

---

[82] Successive Argentine governments have continued to finance part of the costs of the Institute.

[83] According to first-hand witnesses the original idea for the EAI was broached in a meeting between George H. W. Bush and Enrique Iglesias.

activities linked to the series of Presidential Summits of the Americas initiated with the EAI, continued during the Clinton Administration, with active participation from the IDB, ECLAC, and the OAS.

The George W. Bush Administration started in January 2001 with promises of greater attention to the region (exemplified by the early meeting in 2001 between the new U.S. president and President Fox of Mexico, who had been recently elected as well). However, the tragic terrorist attacks of September 11, 2001 reoriented the priorities of the U.S. government.

The FTAA process moved slowly until it came to a halt during the Summit of the Americas in Mar del Plata, Argentina, in May 2005. The presidential debate in that meeting was presented in the press as one in favor of, or against, free-trade. An alternative interpretation is that the debate was about the meaning of the integration of the Americas and the possible dimensions of such integration that would allow the Americas to better interact within the region and with the rest of the world (see Díaz-Bonilla, 2009b).[84] Argentina, as the host country and strongly supported by Brazil and other Latin American countries, proposed jobs and investments as the theme for the Summit. The issue of the completion of the FTAA was left in brackets in the pre-negotiated declaration and the final wording simply reflected that there was no agreement on this topic.

A different way of looking at this debate would be to recognize a) that commerce was increasing in the Americas in any case, with many countries having different types of trade agreements among themselves; and b) that the main constraints to increased economic integration were not necessarily tariffs or the legal issues considered in

---

[84] President George W. Bush made a special reference to the interaction of the Americas with China. In his initial intervention in Mar del Plata he explained that there was a window of opportunity in Congress to advance with the FTAA negotiations, but that window was closing, and therefore it was important to move fast. But the most interesting part was the rationale for the FTAA: President Bush said that it was very important for the Americas to be together, because that was the only way all the countries participating in the Mar del Plata Summit could favorably interact with China and Asia in the global economy (Díaz-Bonilla, 2009b). In fact, the American countries acting together can be significant economic and social players in the global economy considering that they have a population of close to 920 million people and represent about one third of world GDP (2009 data). However, a legitimate debate is whether the FTAA, as it was conceived, is the best way to generate that integration and collective action, or whether other approaches and arrangements may be needed.

the FTAA, but rather i) the existence of serious political and social objections (linked to fears about job losses because of trade liberalization, both in Latin America and the United States), and ii) widespread deficiencies in logistical and infrastructural issues.

In other words, the real debate was not whether there was going to be further integration in the Americas, which had been consistently advancing along different dimensions for many years, and particularly since the mid 1980s. The real question was whether the main requisite for such integration was to establish further legal rules of the type envisaged in the FTAA, or rather, in an approach closer to the conception of the European Union, a key problem was to invest in infrastructure, human capital, safety nets, and social inclusion, all of which was needed to make economic integration more balanced in social and political terms (Díaz-Bonilla, 2009b).[85]

Current and Future Challenges

Looking to the current and future challenges, the operation of the Bank will take place within a framework characterized by two imbalances in the global economy that lack clear coordination mechanisms, but whose evolution carry significant systemic consequences, particularly for the poor and vulnerable (see Díaz-Bonilla, 2008). The first problem, which is more relevant for the short to medium term, relates to the world macroeconomic imbalances at the heart of the current crisis. Global macroeconomic coordination is a central issue of world governance; the lack of a properly coordinated approach has negative implications for poverty alleviation to the extent that it increases the possibility of trade wars, financial crises, and economic recessions.

For the medium to long term, a second key topic of world governance is how to solve the market and institutional failures associated with energy, climate change, natural resources, and food security, with their impact on poverty and health trends in developing countries. Latin America can play an important role among developing regions in the adequate handling of those two imbalances. Support from the IDB and other financial institutions would greatly help in this regard.

---

[85] Also, some of the components of the FTAA, such as the completely free movement of financial capital, had been controversial even in the negotiations with Chile, a country with fairly open international operations.

Regarding the global macroeconomic imbalances, several points may be mentioned. First, although the U.S. current account deficit has come down somewhat after reaching more than 1.6 percent of the *world* GDP in 2006, a level unprecedented in modern history, it is still high. Second, the current policies followed by the industrialized countries up to now may not solve the imbalances and could well in part aggravate them: the main economic stimulus is taking place within the United States, when it should be reducing and not expanding its external deficit, while other countries and regions, which should expand their domestic demand, are trying to export their way out of the current economic recession.

Within that uncertain scenario, Latin America and the Caribbean is playing a positive role by sustaining aggregate demand and helping reduce imbalances at the world level: the region has run moderate trade deficits in 2008/2009 that averaged about 0.6% of the regional GDP per year. It must also be noted that private consumption in Latin America and the Caribbean is larger than in other developing regions: in current dollars of 2008, the region's private consumption is about 17 percent larger than India and China combined (see Díaz-Bonilla, 2009a). Also, from the point of view of the United States, Latin America and the Caribbean is a key export market, with almost 21 percent of U.S. sales going to the region –a similar percentage as the individual shares of Canada and of the European Union (each one separately), and about double all *developing* Asia (including China). Therefore, in terms of the current cycle, and particularly for the United States, it is important to maintain long-term financial flows to the region (as opposed to short term, "hot" money). This would support general economic activity in Latin America and contribute to global aggregate demand. The IDB, by borrowing in countries with excess savings, and lending those funds to Latin American countries for investment purposes, contributes to rebalance global financial and trade flows.

Looking beyond the current cycle, the financial crisis still unfolding is creating a structure of global supply and demand for lending resources that may not be favorable to developing countries: although currently expansionary monetary policies in industrialized countries have increased global liquidity, over time, developed countries' substantial fiscal deficits will put pressure on global financial markets, while the international supply of funds will be restricted by the process of deleveraging and restructuring of the global financial system and the future normalization of monetary policies.[86]

The IDB, as a useful multiplier of development resources, can contribute to alleviating those global imbalances.[87] The reason is that for each dollar paid in cash to the commercial (Ordinary Capital) and concessional (Fund for Special Operations) windows from *all members* during the 1994 capital increase, the value of projects generated in the region by the Bank since that year has reached about 110 dollars by 2009. This multiplier effect has certainly helped the borrowing member countries, but the non-borrowing member countries have also benefited: as a result of the demand generated by the projects financed by IDB, non-borrowing member countries exported to LAC country members of the Bank about 15 dollars for each dollar that the *non-borrowers* invested in cash in the institution.[88] [89]

Turning now to the medium-term issues of energy, agriculture, and climate change, different studies show that while the accumulation of greenhouse gases throughout history has been caused largely by the now developed countries, the adverse impact is being felt more

---

[86] Haldane (2010) and McKinsey Global Institute (2010) provide additional views on the evolution of global savings and investments, with the potential impacts on world real interest rates.

[87] It should be recognized that this contribution is relatively minor because the size of the IDB is small compared to the GDP of the region. For instance, in 2008 and 2009, even though these were record years in IDB's loan approvals, the volume of gross lending (i.e. without subtracting repayments from LAC countries to the Bank) amounted to only about 0.3-0.4 percent of the GDP of Latin America and the Caribbean. The net flows (i.e. discounting the repayments to the Bank) were far smaller. A larger impact would require a larger institution as well, but even considering the current Ninth Capital increase, the size of the Bank will not change much as percentage of the region's GDP.

[88] Currently, the IDB has 48 member countries. There are 26 borrowing member countries: Argentina, the Bahamas, Barbados, Belize, Bolivia, Brazil, Chile, Colombia, Costa Rica, the Dominican Republic, Ecuador, El Salvador, Guatemala, Guyana, Haiti, Honduras, Jamaica, Mexico, Nicaragua, Panama, Paraguay, Peru, Suriname, Trinidad and Tobago, Uruguay and Venezuela. Non-borrowing member countries (22 in total) include: Austria, Belgium, Canada, the People's Republic of China, Croatia, Denmark, Finland, France, Germany, Israel, Italy, Japan, the Republic of Korea, the Netherlands, Norway, Portugal, Slovenia, Spain, Sweden, Switzerland, the United Kingdom, and the United States.

[89] The export values reflect the period 1995-2007, for which complete data exists; adding 2008 and 2009 will certainly increase further the average multiplier of 15:1. These calculations refer only to the Ordinary Capital and the Fund for Special Operations, and do not include other smaller contributions.

dramatically in developing countries, particularly those located in the tropics. In the case of the IDB these problems affect some of the poorer and more vulnerable member countries of the Bank in Central America and the Caribbean. A proper handling of those issues is also affected by a market-coordination failure of global proportions, as forcefully argued in the Stern Report (2006). Then, it seems clear that, for the medium to long term, a key topic of world governance is how to solve the market and institutional failures associated with energy, climate change, environmental issues, and food security. Over time, this global governance issue, will be more relevant for poverty trends in developing countries than the question of how to solve the shorter-term global macroeconomic imbalances.

Latin America is a crucial actor for the proper management of those issues (Díaz-Bonilla, 2009a):

*It is a region with a large availability of freshwater resources (almost 24,500 cubic meters per capita, more than double the average in developed countries and three times the average in developing regions).

*Latin America and the Caribbean generates a significant global trade surplus in agricultural and food products, which from 2005-2007 reached about 52 billion dollars and 36 billion dollars per year on average, respectively; the next group of net suppliers is comprised by four developed countries (United States, Canada, Australia and New Zealand) which have net trade surpluses of about 40 billion dollars (agricultural products) and 33 billion dollars (food products).[90] The rest of the regions and groups of countries have relatively balanced trade positions, or are net importers. Therefore, the Americas plus Australia and New Zealand, basically provide most of the global net trade surplus for agricultural and food items, and the largest percentage comes from Latin America and the Caribbean.[91]

*The region has lower CO2 emissions per unit of GDP (measured in PPP) than both developed and developing countries: 0.32 kg per

---

[90] Data is from FAOSTAT (http://faostat.fao.org), corresponding to the aggregates "Agriculture" and "Food and Animals."

[91] It should be noted that aggregate domestic consumption of agricultural and food products for many countries comes mainly from domestic sources of production, with imports providing a generally smaller complement (typically between 10-20 percent in the aggregate, although the percentages may be far higher for specific commodities). In any case, international trade supplies the margin needed to avoid large swings in domestic availability and prices.

GDP (measured in 2005 PPP dollars) in LAC, against 0.41 in High Income OECD countries, and 0.66 for all developing countries.

*Out of the ten top countries in plant biodiversity at the world level, six are located in the region, including the top two.

*About a quarter of the area of world forests is in Latin America and the Caribbean (some 960 million hectares, out of a world total of 3,870 million hectares, according to the World Resources Institute). The Amazon forest is a crucial source of oxygen for the world.

*The region, as a whole, is a net exporter of energy products, although the net supply to the world is clearly smaller than that of the Middle East. However, for the United States, two out of its four top suppliers are in Latin America, and a third one, Canada, is in the Americas.

Therefore, the region has significant and positive global externalities in most of the dimensions mentioned. Sustaining those positive externalities, while avoiding the negative impacts of climate change on the people of Latin America and the Caribbean, particularly the most vulnerable, requires substantial investments in the next decades. Part of those investments will have to be provided by an expanded IDB. If Latin America cannot confront those challenges adequately and the positive global externalities associated now with the region decline, the negative implications of that potential failure for the rest of the world will be significant.

Countries in Latin America and the Caribbean not only face the traditional challenges of underdevelopment, poverty, and inequality still afflicting the region, but will also have to make additional investments simply to avoid losing ground due to the higher costs of adapting to climate change. Both the financial crisis and global warming are not the result of actions or decisions of countries in the region, yet they are affected now, and will be suffering greater impacts in the future, because of those global developments.

In summary, an expanded IDB must play a role in any solution for the region to address the longstanding problem of underdevelopment as well as the new challenges of the financial crisis and of climate change, which could erase the significant economic, political, and social gains of recent years.

That agenda must be pursued in the context of an expanded program for regional and global economic integration, as mandated in the Ninth Capital increase. Divergences in views between negotiating further legal trade frameworks or focusing on investments and social cohesion seem to have been reduced since discrepancies emerged in Mar del Plata in 2005.

Most member countries of the IDB are focusing on investments in infrastructure, human capital, poverty alleviation, and social inclusion, among the more traditional issues, as well as sustainable energy, and climate adaptation and mitigation. All these topics are part of a new positive agenda for integration in the Americas, but also opened to IDB's member countries from Europe and Asia. In particular, the European Union's approach, with its focus on, among other things, infrastructure, regional balances, and social cohesion, has much to offer to the countries of Latin America and the Caribbean. An expanded IDB will have an important role in the implementation of such approach.

c) International Structures and Governance: Resources

Historical Perspectives

A third broad topic mentioned at the beginning of this chapter relates to the history of the interaction between Latin America and the United States in the construction of international structures of governance, including the issues of democratic decision making and burden sharing within those structures. A recurrent objective of Latin American countries has been to keep the United States engaged in the region through a) more symmetrical trade and financial links, and b) multilateral security arrangements that protected the region from external threats while at the same time limited the possibility of unilateral interventions by the United States (or by any other powerful country).

The negotiations related to the successive proposals for regional banks show the search of Latin American countries for a more equal relationship with the United States, mostly through pooling resources and shared decision making. For instance, the International American Bank of 1890 would have been open to private investors both from the United States and Latin America; the Inter-American Bank of 1940 considered a majority of shares from Latin American countries, as it was the case of the finally created Inter-American Development Bank (although a majority of the widely usable resources, particularly in the concessional windows, has come from the United States).

In fact, the ownership structure was one of the reasons why the last two institutions generated resistances from some U.S. groups that disliked putting resources in an institution not completely controlled by that country.

At the same time, although Latin American countries wanted responsibility in the regional bank and were also ready to put serious money into it, they also considered that a regional financial institution without the United States would not function properly. Therefore, Latin Americans wanted the United States to be the single most important contributor, but, at the same time, they expected that the U.S. share did not exceed that of the LAC countries as a whole.

These ideas about burden sharing were in line with the convictions of the Eisenhower Administration: the fact that Latin America contributed important resources to the new institution was consistent both with the need for self-reliance (which Eisenhower officials persistently advocated to the region), and with the importance the U.S. government gave to fiscal discipline at home (which precluded an open-ended financial commitment to the new institution by the United States).

In the end, it generated IDB's structure of "borrowers-as-owners" that has distinguished the Bank from other institutions and helped maintain a long-term development agenda in the region. In that regard, Latin America and the Caribbean has been successful: for instance Krasner (1981), comparing the three regional development banks, has argued that "in the Inter-American Development Bank developing country members have secured both influence and resources, in the Asian Development Bank they have secured resources but little influence, and in the African Development Bank they have influence but little resources" (p. 304).

In any case, the dialogue and controversies about how to balance influence and resources have been a permanent fact of life in the history of the IDB.

Looking at the issue of allocation and use of resources as a whole, several points may be highlighted. First, it has already been pointed out that a majority of the resources of the Bank paid in cash in the Ordinary Capital comes from the borrowing member countries. Also, in the concessional windows, although the United States has been historically the main contributor, the Bank has shown greater levels of solidarity intra-developing countries than other multilateral development banks. For instance, the last important replenishment of the FSO in 1998 was done basically with money from the borrowing member countries.[92]

---

[92] The mechanism was the conversion of local currency holdings by borrowing member countries (which according to IDB's Charter each one could use for its own

The next Table 1 shows the percentages of the contributions to the concessional windows for IDA and the three regional banks, divided according to whether they come from non-borrowers, borrowers or income transfers from the ordinary capital of those institutions.[93] Data is accumulated until 2008 and refers to effectively paid contributions (not pledged).

TABLE 1

	Concessional Funds: Total Contributions		
	Borrowers	Non Borrowers	Transfers from Income
IDB[1]	26.4%	73.6%	0.0%
AfDB[2]	0.1%	97.6%	2.3%
AsDB[3]	0.2%	97.3%	2.6%
IDA[4]	2.4%	90.3%	7.2%

Sources:

[1] Inter-American Development Bank Annual Report 2008, pp. 81, Annex II-3, 4th column.

[2] African Development Bank Annual Report 2008, pp. 211, Note O, 6th column.

[3] Asian Development Bank Annual Report 2008, pp. 80, Note ADF-6, 5th column.

[4] The World Bank Annual Report 2009, pp. 136-138, 3rd. column. The Report shows *pledged* contributions. To make it comparable with the other institutions, we transformed pledged contributions into *paid-in* contributions by assuming that the percentages from Borrowers and non Borrowers are the same in paid-in and pledged contributions. Transfer from Income includes a 1,100 million dollars grant from IFC.

---

purposes), into hard currency resources that were assigned to the FSO to be used only by the poorer countries.

[93] Because borrowing member countries own a larger percentage of the Ordinary Capital of the Bank, transfers from the income generated by that capital would imply as well a larger percentage of contributions from borrowers to the concessional window.

It is clear from Table 1 that borrowing member countries at the IDB have contributed far more to the concessional window than borrowers in other multilateral development banks, irrespective of whether there are transfers from the income of the ordinary capital of the banks or not.[94] Now the Ninth Capital increase includes a transfer of funds (in grant form) to Haiti from the Ordinary Capital for about 2,200 million dollars during eleven years, and all the previous FSO debt of that country has been condoned. This is another clear display of solidarity among borrowing member countries, considering that the money will come from the greater interest rates those countries will have to pay on their loans in order to finance the transfers.

Second, in addition to analyzing the source of funds it is important to also look at their uses. Table 2 presents net capital flows to borrowing countries using two different categories applied by the IDB: countries A (the larger and richest ones in the region), and D (the poorer ones); and Group I (relatively higher income countries in the region) and II (relatively lower income ones).[95] [96] It also considers two measures: net capital flow as percentage of the GDP of the borrowing countries and in per capita terms. The data shows yearly averages per type of country and indicators.

---

[94] In particular, not counting the United States (which represents about 50 percent of the value of the contributions to the concessional window, mainly because of the large U.S. payments during the earlier decades of the IDB), LAC countries have contributed more to the concessional windows than all the other non-borrowing member countries combined.

[95] The Department of Finance of the IDB publishes data on net flows between the Bank and the borrowing member countries since 1975. The data used is called "Net Capital Flow" and considers disbursements to the countries minus repayments of principal to the Bank, and minus subscriptions and contributions paid by the countries.

[96] Group A: Argentina, Brazil, Mexico, Venezuela; Group B: Chile, Colombia, Peru; Group C: Bahamas, Barbados, Costa Rica, Jamaica, Panama, Surinam, Trinidad and Tobago, Uruguay; Group D: Belize, Bolivia, Dominican Republic, Ecuador, El Salvador, Guatemala, Guyana, Haiti, Honduras, Nicaragua, Paraguay. Group I: Argentina, Bahamas, Barbados, Brazil, Chile, Mexico, Trinidad and Tobago, Uruguay, Venezuela. Group II: Belize, Bolivia, Colombia, Costa Rica, Dominican Republic, Ecuador, El Salvador, Guatemala, Guyana, Haiti, Honduras, Jamaica, Nicaragua, Panama, Paraguay, Peru, Suriname. The seven countries A and B represent about 86% of total GDP and 80% of total population in LAC.

TABLE 2

Net Flows from the IDB (annual averages)		
	1975/2007	2000s
As percent of GDP		
A countries	0.06	0.03
D countries	0.62	0.39
Group I countries	0.07	0.03
Group II countries	0.39	0.23
Per capita (US dollars)		
A countries	2.2	1.1
D countries	6.2	5.8
Group I countries	2.3	1.1
Group II countries	5.2	4.8
Source: Author's calculations from IDB data		

Table 2 clearly shows that the IDB has benefitted the smaller and poorer borrowing countries substantially more than the bigger and richer ones, although all have received financial support. The differences are more marked when using transfers as percentage of the GDP (5-10 times more support to Group II compared to Group I), but still in per capita terms the preference for smaller and poorer countries is clear (about 2-5 times more support, depending on the periods considered). This reflects in numbers the fact highlighted by Enrique Iglesias in his farewell speech as president of the IDB: "the culture of solidarity [at the Bank] has been preserving the rights of the small countries since the beginning" (Iglesias, 2005).

Another point to be noted is that there have been several instances during the last years in which, mostly at the initiative of LAC countries, the IDB was able to face important challenges with its own resources and without having to ask the United States and other non-borrowing member countries for additional funds. One such case was the debt relief in 2007 under the Multilateral Debt Relief Initiative, where the idea of using a blend of resources from Ordinary

Capital and FSO to provide debt relief was suggested by some LAC countries.[97] Also most of the financial engineering utilized to increase lending by the Bank during the current global financial crisis, including the idea of a temporary callable capital that was eventually provided by Canada, was first proposed by LAC shareholders.[98] Those measures were then implemented by the IDB during the period 2008 to 2010 to help the region without having to increase the capital base.

In summary, despite having their own problems of underdevelopment and poverty, borrowing member countries of the IDB have contributed significant amounts of funds to this institution not only as the main generators of net income, but also, and crucially, as contributors of cash capital to a Bank. Also they have supported an operational approach that has given preference to smaller and poorer countries, showing strong South-South regional solidarity. Finally, they have proactively contributed ideas to optimize IDB's resources, which delayed the need for a capital increase. However, as the IDB has stepped up its lending in response to the recent financial crisis, the Bank reached the limits of what financial engineering could do and the Ninth Capital Increase had to be negotiated. In those negotiations the topics of influence and resources raised by Krasner (1981) have been again part of the debate.

Current and Future Challenges

The current capital increase for the IDB is taking place during a period in which the United States and other industrial countries members of the Bank have their attention focused on other areas: there are military problems in the Middle East and Asia; poverty is more evident in Africa and in broad swaths of developing Asia; and the current economic crisis has negatively affected growth and fiscal and

---

[97] The original proposal was presented by Argentina and Haiti. It suggested a combination of loans from the Ordinary Capital and from the Fund of Special Operations to ensure the continuation of lending to the poorer countries even after granting them debt relief, and without having to ask member countries for additional funds to compensate the FSO for the funds used to pardon the debt. An important IDB non-borrowing member country made clear at that time that it was not prepared to allocate funds to compensate the FSO for the debt relief exercise, and therefore the only way to reduce the debt of the poorer countries was through the mechanism suggested by those LAC countries.

[98] One of the authors of this book was directly involved in originating the financial proposals.

employment indicators in industrialized countries. Although with differences across countries, Latin America and the Caribbean is again considered to be in relatively better shape than other developing regions –with many of the countries in the region regarded as members of an emerging global middle class. Therefore, the region and the IDB are not necessarily among the top priorities for the industrialized countries that provide the bulk of the resources for the international financial institutions as a whole.

On the other hand, the World Bank and the African and Asian Development Banks lend to relatively poorer countries and, therefore, these institutions receive more attention and resources. Governments in developed countries may well consider that asking their own taxpayers to contribute to these international institutions in the middle of the current deep crisis may only be done if it is presented as helping solely those countries suffering from extreme poverty –a situation that, with exceptions, is more prevalent in developing regions other than Latin America and the Caribbean.

Therefore, to maintain the interest of the United States and other developed countries in the region and the IDB what is needed is to highlight, paraphrasing John Kennedy, "not what the world can do for Latin America, but what Latin America can do for the world" (Díaz-Bonilla, 2009a). As argued before, such an argument should be based on the positive contributions of Latin America and the Caribbean to a) the reduction of global macroeconomic imbalances; b) a better global management of energy, environmental, and food security issues; and c) the spread of democracy (Díaz-Bonilla, 2009a).

Even if the interest of IDB's industrialized members in the region is maintained, borrowing and non-borrowing countries may have different views on what is the best way to use the return to their capital invested in the Bank. Some non-borrowing countries are concerned that the returns on that capital may be used to "subsidize" middle-income countries through low interest rates, and they would rather increase the income of the Bank and use it to finance transfers to the concessional windows for the poorer countries.

On the other hand, borrowing member countries, who contribute more than half of the paid-in capital, argue that the low loan spread charged by the IDB until recently merely reflected global market conditions; that with the blended loans resulting from the 2007 debt relief (as explained before), low interest rates in the operations funded with the Ordinary Capital also benefit those countries that use the concessional window (FSO); and that increasing interest rates to maximize returns on the Ordinary Capital (which would then be transferred to the FSO window) places the burden of helping the poorest countries in the region only on middle-income borrowing member countries who have clearly lower incomes per capita than IDB's non-borrowing shareholders.[99] Also, transfers to the concessional windows from the income from Ordinary Capital have a negative multiplier effect on potential approvals and disbursements in the future, which may make those transfers a less efficient instrument for the Bank as a whole, than direct contributions.[100] Finally, it has been shown before that IDB's operations generate clear differences in net flows of capital per capita and per GDP in favor of smaller and poorer countries.[101]

Going forward however, a strong case can be made about the importance that LAC countries take increased financial responsibility in this Bank using their own resources. It is true that, as argued in previous chapters, Latin America tried for many decades to convince the United States to join a regional bank and support it with additional funds. Also, LAC countries have always very much appreciated the participation in the Bank of other non-borrowing partners that have joined the institution since the early 1970s. The multiple intellectual and financial contributions they have brought to the Bank are deeply valued. In that sense, the IDB is a partnership (similar to a cooperative in many regards) in which all countries benefit on different dimensions. In particular, for non-borrowing member countries, there

---

[99] The accumulated paid-in capital before the current capital increase has reached approximately 4 billion dollars; the Ninth Capital increase will add 1.7 billion dollars to that previous number.

[100] Under current financial ratios, each dollar of annual transfers of OC income toward any utilization other than accumulation of reserves translates into a smaller future *stock* of outstanding loans to the region of about three dollars (i.e. there will be fewer loans from the Bank to the region because of the transfer). If we consider approvals (i.e. we move from stocks to *flows*), the ratio of losses is about seven dollars less in approvals per one dollar less in reserves over ten years. This makes the agreement to support Haiti even more remarkable as a demonstration of intra-developing countries solidarity, considering the reduction in the level of lending to other countries it implies.

[101] There is also an implicit administrative subsidy going from large projects (which usually take place in larger countries) to smaller projects (which are more common in smaller countries). This is so because, normally, the adequate preparation of a project requires a level of technical and operational effort that does not diminish with the size of the operation (i.e. smaller projects are more expensive per dollar lent).

are at least two positive outcomes: a) one is the importance of contributing to political stability and democracy in the region, avoiding or minimizing negative spillovers on their own societies in a globalized world (such as health problems, illegal immigration, international crime, environmental problems, and so on); and b) there are also economic advantages related to their exports to LAC countries that materialize as a result of IDB projects (as argued before). Even without the positive outcomes mentioned, there is always the moral and ethical argument compelling all human beings to help fight poverty and exclusion.

Having said that, LAC countries cannot expect, nor should they seek or want, recurrent financial contributions on the part of the non-borrowing partners at the Bank. LAC countries should take primary responsibility for the region, focusing especially on the poorer and more vulnerable people and societies, as it has been increasingly happening over the last decades. The main contribution that may be needed from non-borrowing member countries will be to increase the callable (or guarantee capital) from time to time.[102]

In any case, the expansion of the IDB and its future operations must be conducted in a respectful dialogue in which the borrowing and non-borrowing member countries can learn and act together. We discuss these issues next.

d) International Structures and Governance: Dialogue, Learning, and Consensus

Historical Perspectives

Another fact that emerges from the historical narrative is the two-way (but not symmetric) influences in the dialogue in the Americas, which has been properly characterized as one of the longest running examples of such regional interaction (Domínguez, 2007). The United

---

[102] The guarantee of the "callable capital" has never been invoked to cover IDB's obligations in the more than 50 years of operations of the institution. In fact, Latin American countries have the greatest interest in that the guarantee of the callable capital is never utilized: first, because having to exercise the guarantee will most likely affect the triple A financial rating of the institution; and, second, because if the guarantee is invoked *all* countries have to pay (and not only the industrialized countries). Therefore, and notwithstanding different budgetary and accounting rules in IDB's member countries, the cost of callable capital for the non-borrowing member countries is very low or nil.

States learned and experimented many institutional and policy approaches in its contacts with the Latin American republics. Ideas flowed both ways and agreements and compromises emerged – although, inevitably, in many cases views differed about whether there was a fair balance across the interests of the countries involved.

Based on those regional exchanges the United States, in several instances, projected the experiences to world affairs when its interests became more global after World War I and, particularly, since World War II. This was clearly the case of the 1940 Inter-American Bank as the predecessor of the Bretton Woods institutions. But, before this example, it was also the case of the 1919 League of Nations, whose principles were presented by Woodrow Wilson in an Inter-American Conference in 1916 and the negotiations started in the region. Several decades later, the example of the Rio Treaty as a precedent for NATO can also be mentioned.

The pattern of regional learning and experimentation is explained by the timing of the political formation of all the American republics and by the geographical proximity. This intense regional interaction continued for some time, but it had an inflexion point around the end of World War II, when U.S. interests became truly global. Once the war was over, U.S. international policy learning and experimentation happened in many fronts, of which LAC, during long stretches of time, was not necessarily the most important one of them. After that, the attention of the United States to the region was mostly linked to crises that emerged from time to time.

LAC countries, which had been used to a strong and profound interaction with the United States (interaction that was also highly contentious at times), began to feel neglected, starting with Truman in the late 1940s. During those times, Latin America was perceived by the U.S. government to be in better shape and, therefore, in less need of U.S. support than other parts of the world. However, the advances of the Soviet Union and the social turmoil in the region, made evident by the events marring Vice-President Nixon's trip to the region in 1958, prompted a correction in the Eisenhower Administration's perception of the region. It also led to the creation of the IDB.

This period was later extended by the Alliance for Progress during the Kennedy Administration. But the conceptual framework for the IDB and the Alliance was generated in a not minor way by the interaction with thinkers and politicians from Latin America and the Caribbean: the Mexican proposal in 1940; ECLA since 1948 and, particularly, after the 1949 Havana conference; the 1954 Quitandinha conference in Rio; the work by the group of LAC experts in Santiago, Chile, in 1955; and Kubitschek's "Operación Panamérica," supported by other presidents of the region. The Alliance for Progress also marked the highest point of Prebisch's interaction with, and influence on, policy-making circles in the United States (Dosman, 2008).

LAC's quest to keep the United States engaged in the region through more symmetric relations and the desire to influence the U.S. decision-making process in that dialogue, as well as the issue of the balance between influence and resources in such relationship did not end, of course, with the creation of the IDB. The Alliance for Progress saw an expansion of U.S. funds to the Bank and the creation and operation of different inter-American bodies for regional consultations and decision making.

With the decline of the Alliance, the United States began to diminish the percentage of its contributions to the IDB, and promoted the incorporation of European countries and Japan in the mid 1970s (which also reduced the need for Latin American contributions). Latin American countries, as well as Ortiz Mena who carefully orchestrated the expansion of IDB's membership, expected that the new structure would help the region to better manage the Bank under what then became a triangular relationship with the United States and those new members. But it is also true that the Nixon Administration wanted both to reduce its own financial contributions and to have other potential allies in the industrialized countries that were joining the Bank, while Latin America reduced its shares (and, therefore, voting power) to accommodate the countries joining the IDB.

The political controversies during the 1980s around the situation in Nicaragua and Central America in general, and the differences about the economic policies needed to deal with the debt crises in LAC, led to divisions among IDB's shareholders. LAC countries, with about 55 percent of the votes at that time, used their majority voting power to prevail in some decisions, against the opinion of the United States and other non-borrowing member countries. The United States wanted to have additional institutional means within the Board of Executive Directors to block decisions it did not like.

Because the Bank was also running out of resources in the second half of the 1980s, the complicated negotiations for the Seventh capital increase during the late 1980s brokered a compromise through which two or more Directors could postpone the treatment of a project for up to twelve months. From the point of view of the United States this agreement enforced a significant waiting period for projects that it opposed. For Latin American countries this agreement preserved the voting power contemplated in the constitution of the Bank and did not give the United States or the non-borrowing countries veto power in the operations of the Ordinary Capital.[103]

It was also agreed that the IDB was going to expand its lending into a different type of projects, with macroeconomic and sectoral policy conditionality, under the tutelage of the IMF and the World Bank.[104]

The counterpart was an increase of somewhat more than 75 percent in the capital of the Bank, which allowed the lending program to increase from an annual average of about 2,200 million dollars in the 10 years prior to the capital increase to a potential lending level of somewhat more than 5,000 million dollars per year afterwards (Inter-American Development Bank, 2006).

The George H.W. Bush and Clinton Administrations in the late 1980s and during the 1990s opened a new period of U.S. positive attention to, and interaction with, Latin America and the Caribbean, with beneficial implications for the functioning of the IDB.

The 1994 Eight Capital replenishment increased the Ordinary Capital of the Bank by about two thirds and the Fund for Special Operations received an additional amount of 1,000 million dollars, which would transform the Bank into the main source of development funding for the region. The special decision-making procedure approved during the Seventh capital increase (that was never used) and the explicit tutelage from the World Bank and the IMF were dropped. At the same time, the non-regional, non-borrowing member countries, and Canada, expanded their voting power to almost 20 percent of total shares (Inter-American Development Bank, 2006). Latin American and Caribbean countries, which had about 60 percent of the shares when the IDB was created, reduced progressively their share to the present level of barely above 50 percent. This voting structure allows the region to retain a majority, but also places borrowing member

---

[103] On the other hand, as it has been already mentioned, the United States has veto power regarding FSO projects.

[104] As discussed before, both the envisaged policies and the subordinated role of the IDB vis-à-vis the Bretton Woods institutions was a major point of contention between the United States and LAC countries, and one of the reasons for the resignation of Antonio Ortiz Mena.

countries always at the edge of not being able to hold those votes together. On the other hand, the United States declined from 40 percent to about 30 percent, retaining its veto power on several key decisions, such as approval of FSO projects and the formation of quorum at meetings of the Board of Governors.

In any case, this special structure of ownership, with almost equal voting power between borrowing and non-borrowing member countries, has highlighted the importance of forging consensus on most key issues. This has been very positive for the IDB. Enrique Iglesias in his farewell speech as president of the IDB, on September 29, 2005, noted that "the Bank possesses great assets. An enviable financial strength; the confidence of the Member countries, which to a great extent is based on the feeling of 'ownership' of the borrowing member countries, and a model of consensus internalized in its institutional culture that allows solid and lasting decisions…[Consensus] takes time and creates some frustrations. But in an institution like this, where there are countries so different in their economic and financial power, achieving consensus is a way of ensuring the participation of the smallest and weakest members" (Iglesias, 2005).

The governance structure of the Bank is also special due to other reasons, such as the fact that the president of the institution is elected through open competition within LAC countries. Also, the composition of the staff of the Bank, particularly at the top management jobs, reflects the ownership structure, with a strong presence of personnel from borrowing member countries. Moreover, because the developing countries from Latin America and the Caribbean have contributed substantial resources to the institution, all incentives are aligned to avoid free riders and to elicit collective responsibility among borrowing member countries.

As importantly, this structure of ownership has allowed the Bank to be attentive to the needs and requests of the region, which has also led to innovative approaches in its operations. For instance, while fears of acquiring the reputation of a "universal soup kitchen" (a criticism raised by the Financial Times in December 1946; see Kapur et al, 1997, p. 76) and potential credit rating problems kept the World Bank away from funding social projects, since the beginning the IDB took those challenges head on. Felipe Herrera's holistic vision of development was not limited to the economic field; his "bank of ideas" was the first to support projects then considered to have low returns. In topics such as water and sanitation, education, urban development, and health the IDB pioneered loans to sectors in ways that proved to be compatible with sound banking practices. The World Bank, which with its early presidents had avoided social development projects, eventually started to fund this type of projects as well.

During the 1960s the Bank also supported national science and technology councils, national planning offices and development banks, and promoted the modernization of universities (Inter-American Development Bank, 2001). In the 1970s and early 1980s, innovation happened on different fronts. An example was the encouragement of institutional development through global loans for multiple works and general balance-of-payment financing of industrial inputs, which anticipated in part, but without the same policy conditionality, what was called later structural adjustment loans.[105] Export financing had from the start been both a regional goal and a controversial subject with the non-borrowing member countries; but the IDB was finally able to expand those programs thanks to the Venezuelan Fund, generously funded by that country in 1975 for 500 million (somewhat more than 2,000 million dollars in March 2010 currency). Innovations in non-conventional loans included a tourism project in 1971 that developed Cancún, a project proposal that had been previously rejected by the World Bank. There were also efforts at targeting the conservation of cultural heritage. Other initiatives included small loans to microenterprises, a pioneering activity that anticipated in many years what was later called microfinance.

After the oil shock in the 1970s the Bank supported alternative energy projects that were a novelty at the time, such as geothermal energy in Costa Rica. The IDB was also the first institution to adopt an environmental policy; projects such as reforestation initiatives in Nicaragua were groundbreaking developments in multilateral financing.

During the 1990s, with the advance of democracy, the IDB focused on the fundamental importance of sound, well-functioning institutions for development, and made significant contributions towards it. Projects aimed at modernizing state institutions covered a wide array of areas, such as executive, legislative, and judicial reforms, decentralization assistance, and fiscal and financial sector

---

[105] We are indebted to Enrique García, current President of the "Corporación Andina de Fomento" (CAF), for explaining us these operations that he helped to develop when he was a member of the IDB staff.

reforms. The aim has been to improve capacity building and accountability of the public sector, while strengthening civil society. Citizen security became also a new area of innovative work.

The Bank also expanded during the 1990s a variety of activities related to the private sector, particularly through the creation of the Multilateral Investment Fund (FOMIN in Spanish), an original instrument that opened new avenues of work with the civil society.

In summary, the Bank's close links to the region and the status of member countries as "owners" led the institution to focus its attention on the region's needs, ensured that one-size-fits-all policies were largely avoided, and promoted experimentation and innovation.

Current and Future Challenges

Today at the IDB, as it happened both before and after its creation, the debate continues about the double question of a) what type of Bank we want; and b) what type of society we want to build with the help of the IDB.

Regarding the first question, there are different issues to consider. For instance, do we want a bank divided between "donors," on the one hand, which assign money and then expect to determine conditions and establish controls, and "beneficiaries," on the other, who depend on the money and decisions of other people? Or would we rather continue to strengthen a bank of partners who, in respectful dialogue and with a fair burden sharing in the contribution of resources try to build together expanding spaces of civilized societies to the benefit of all member countries?

Do we want a bank that under the flawed argument of "division of labor" with other international financial institutions may see diluted its own institutional and fiduciary responsibilities, while at the same time the necessary competition of ideas and approaches may be significantly reduced? Or do we prefer an IDB that, of course, coordinates with other financial institutions, but that such coordination is done recognizing the central role of the Bank in the region due to the breadth and depth of its work experience there and its attention and adaptation to the highly changing needs of its individual member countries?

From the point of view of the free flow of ideas, there should not be an institutional monopoly on issues and approaches. In this regard, the presence of the IDB ensures that other views, many of them from the region, are heard. In any case, and considering now financial aspects, the needs in the region, as noted by countless Latin Americans in the debates leading to the creation of the IDB, are large enough to allow for more than one institutional provider of financial resources. It is clear that for LAC countries the IDB is the main international entity for the financing of development and social inclusion in the region.

Another point to be noticed is the potential contribution of IDB's example in the important debate taking place in the G-20 and other international fora about how to make the global decision-making more legitimate, by giving a larger stake to developing countries in the management of our integrated world. In the case of financial institutions, an option that seems to be receiving the largest attention is to expand the participation of developing countries in the voting structure of the World Bank and the IMF. However, a complementary approach should be to strengthen the institutions that are already more participatory and with a strong presence of developing countries, as it is clearly the case of the IDB. The Bank has a more balanced governance structure than other international institutions, with developing countries having voice and vote and, as a result, greater accountability and commitment to the institution. Moreover, since the expansion of democracy in the region, the links between people and the governments that hold the voting power at the Bank have been reinforced. A more legitimate international financial architecture requires that institutions like the IDB (with a participatory and consensus-based internal decision making process and democratic member countries) reinforce their status rather than trying to subordinate their decisions to what other institutions do.

The second question mentioned was what type of society we want to build. Do we want to define IDB's objectives only in terms of reduction of poverty, inequality, and social exclusion? Or do we want to apply a more comprehensive vision of economic and social development, based on the construction of modern societies with a large middle class and social cohesion and inclusion?

The objectives of reducing poverty, inequity, and social exclusion are indeed very important. Poverty and inequality affect the dignity and full development of human beings, as forcefully argued by John Paul II (1987) and others. They are also the underlying causes of many problems affecting developing countries, including societal violence, political instability, environmental damage, spread of disease, forced migrations, and domestic and transnational crime and terrorism. These dysfunctional effects on the societies affected, both within and outside the region, would be sufficient to justify putting poverty and inequality at the heart of the work of the Bank. It is also important to acknowledge that, whatever the internal problems that developing countries in Latin America and the Caribbean still experience in those dimensions, they are being aggravated by the financial crisis and global warming, both caused in large measure by actions and decisions external to the region.

At the same time, the vision of LAC countries about their own development has always included, but also transcended, an approach focusing solely on poverty and inequality. Various studies have shown that the current "middle class" in many LAC countries is not far above the global poverty standard of two dollars per day and that its members suffer significant fluctuations around that level during their lifetimes, getting in and out of poverty. Therefore, a crucial objective of integrated development is to create dynamic societies in which those below the poverty line are steadily absorbed into an ever expanding middle class. In other words, from the perspective of LAC countries, the objectives of reducing and eliminating poverty, inequality, and social exclusion have been always framed within a larger vision of development. That vision aims at the construction of societies with modern economic structures, decent jobs, large middle classes, democratic participation, solidarity and equity, and sustainability from the point of view of the use of energy and the environment in ways that respond to their own needs.

Not only the people from Latin America and the Caribbean but also those from IDB's non-borrowing partners will benefit from a world in which the region achieves that vision and fulfills those hopes. The IDB, as an institution that is "more than a bank," must be there to help.

Bibliography

Alberdi, Juan Bautista. 1844. "Memoria sobre la conveniencia y objetos de un Congreso Jeneral (sic) Americano." in "Obras Completas" Tomo II. Pages 389-412. Buenos Aires. Imprenta "La Tribuna Nacional." Bolivar 38. 1886
http://books.google.com/books?id=p_KgAAAAMAAJ&printsec=front cover&source=gbs_book_other_versions#v=onepage&q=congreso&f= false

The Bankers Magazine. 1920. "The work of the International High Commission." Volume C. January to June 1920.
Available at
http://www.archive.org/stream/bankersmagazine100cambuoft#page/n4 /mode/1up

Bassett Moore, John. 1920. "The Pan-American Financial Conferences and the Inter-American High Commission." The American Journal of International Law, Vol.14, No. 3, July, pp. 343-355.

Bethel, Leslie and Ian Roxborough. 1988. "Latin America between the Second World War and the Cold War: Some reflections on the 1945-8 Conjuncture." Journal of Latin American Studies, Vol. 20, No. 1, May, pp. 167-189.

Birdsall, Nancy. 2003. "Why It Matters Who Runs the IMF and the World Bank." Center for Global Development, Working Paper Number 22, October 2003. Washington D.C.

Bordo, Michael D. and Anna Schwartz. 2001. "From the Exchange Stabilization Fund to the International Monetary Fund." NBER Working Paper No. W8100, January. Available at
http://www.nber.org/papers/w8100.pdf?new_window=1

Bouzas, Roberto and Peter Knaack. 2009 "The IDB and Half a Century of Regional Integration in Latin America and the Caribbean." Integration and Trade. Volume 13. Number 29. January-June 2009. p.15-26. INTAL/IDB.

Broide, Julio. 1961. "Banco Interamericano de Desarrollo. Sus antecedentes y creación." Banco Interamericano de Desarrollo, Washington, D.C.

Cafiero, Antonio. 2009. Personal communication with Eugenio Díaz-Bonilla.

Charter of Punta del Este. 1961. Available online at http://avalon.law.yale.edu/20th_century/intam16.asp

Collado, Emilio. 1971. Oral History Interview with Emilio Collado, New York, NY, July 7, 1971, by Theodore A. Wilson and Richard McKinzie. Harry S. Truman Library and Museum. Available at http://www.trumanlibrary.org/oralhist/collado1.htm

Collado, Emilio. 1974 Oral History Interview with Emilio Collado, New York, NY, July 11, 1974, by Richard McKinzie. Harry S. Truman Library and Museum.
http://www.trumanlibrary.org/oralhist/collado2.htm

Comas, Xavier. 2000. "Los orígenes del BID. De Unión Monetaria a Banco de Desarrollo. La persistencia de un ideal: la integración económica continental." Asociación de Jubilados del Banco Interamericano de Desarrollo, Washington D.C.

Conferencias Internacionales Americanas 1889-1936. 1938. Dotación Carnegie para la Paz Internacional, Washington, D.C. Available at http://biblio2.colmex.mx/coinam/coinam_1889_1936/base2.htm

Costa Couto, Ronaldo. 1999. "A História Viva do BID e o Brasil." Banco Interamericano de Desarrollo, Washington D.C.

Declaration of Punta del Este. 1961. Available online at http://avalon.law.yale.edu/20th_century/intam15.asp

Dell, Sidney. 1972. "The Inter-American Development Bank: a study in development financing." Praeger Editors, New York.

Díaz-Bonilla, Eugenio. 2008. "Global Macroeconomic Developments and Poverty." IFPRI Discussion Paper No. 00766. International Food Policy Research Institute. May 2008. Washington. DC.

Diaz-Bonilla, Eugenio. 2009a. "Do Not Ask What The World Can Do For Latin America, But What Latin America Can Do For The World, And Then Increase The Capital Of The Inter-American Development Bank." RGE MONITOR, March 24. Available Online at http://www.roubini.com/emergingmarkets-monitor/256125/the_g-20_and_the_iadb

Diaz-Bonilla, Eugenio. 2009b. "Mr. Obama Heads South (Geographically Speaking, Of Course…)." RGE MONITOR, April 20. Available Online at http://www.roubini.com/latam-monitor/256461/mr__obama_heads_south__geographically_speaking__of_course____

Dominguez, Jorge. 2007. "International cooperation in Latin America: the design of regional institutions by slow accretion." In Crafting Cooperation: International Institutions in Comparative Perspective. Amitav Acharya and Alastair Iain Johnston (Eds). Cambridge University Press. 2007

Dosman, Edgard. 2008. "The Life and Times of Raul Prebisch, 1901-1986." McGill-Queens University Press.

Dale, Edwin L. Jr. 1958. "Captain of Our Economic Campaign." The New York Times, Aug. 31,pp. SM8.

Eichengreen, Barry. 1996. "Globalising Capital: A History of the International Monetary System." Princeton University Press, Princeton NJ.

Eisenhower, Dwight. 1958a. Correspondence between Presidents Eisenhower and Kubitschek. June 5, 1958. Available at Woolley, John T. and Gerhard Peters. The American Presidency Project: http://www.presidency.ucsb.edu/ws/index.php?pid=11089

Eisenhower, Dwight. 1958b. Correspondence between Presidents Eisenhower and Frondizi. July 1, 1958. Available at Woolley, John T. and Gerhard Peters. The American Presidency Project: http://www.presidency.ucsb.edu/ws/?pid=11123

Eisenhower, Dwight. 1958c. Speech of President Eisenhower to General Assembly of the United Nations. August 13, 1958. Available at http://www.eisenhowermemorial.org/speeches/19580813%20Third%20Special%20Emergency%20Session%20of%20the%20General%20Assembly%20of%20the%20United%20Nations.htm

Eisenhower, Dwight. 1960. President Eisenhower's press Conference in Newport, RI. *July 11, 1960*. Available at Woolley, John T. and Gerhard Peters. The American Presidency Project: http://www.presidency.ucsb.edu/ws/?pid=11871

Escudé, Carlos and Andrés Cisneros. 2000. "Las inversiones fijas alemanas en la Argentina, en Historia de las Relaciones Exteriores en Argentina." Available at http://www.argentina-rree.com/9/9-035.htm

Federal Reserve. 1940. The Inter-American Bank. Bulletin of the Board of Governors of the Federal Reserve System, Vol. 26, June, pp 517-525. Also available online at http://fraser.stlouisfed.org/publications/FRB/1940/download/53094/frb _061940.pdf

Frieden, Jeff. 1988. "Sectoral Conflict and Foreign Economic Policy, 1914-1940." International Organization, Vol. 42, No. 1, The State and American Foreign Policy, Winter.

Green, David. 1971. "The containment of Latin America: a history of the myths and realities of the good neighbor policy." Quadrangle Books Editors. 1971

Haldane, Andrew G. 2010. "Global imbalances in retrospect and prospect" Speech by Mr Andrew G Haldane, Executive Director, Financial Stability, Bank of England, at the Global Financial Forum, Chatham House Conference on "The New Global Economic Order", London, 3 November 2010. http://www.bis.org/review/r101223f.pdf?frames=0

Helleiner, Eric. 2006. "Reinterpreting Bretton Woods: International Development and the Neglected Origins of Embedded Liberalism." Development and Change 37(5), pp. 943-67.

Helleiner, Eric. 2009a. "Central Bankers as Good Neighbors: U.S. Money Doctors in Latin America During the 1940s." *Financial History Review* 16(1), pp. 1-21.

Helleiner, Eric. 2009b. "The Development Mandate of International Institutions: Where Did It Come From?" Studies in Comparative International Development 44, pp. 189-211.

Horsefield, J. Keith. 1969. Chapter: The Keynes and White Plans (1941-42) in "The International Monetary Fund 19745-1965. Twenty Years of International Monetary Cooperation." Volume 1: Chronicle. International Monetary Fund, Washington, D.C.

Iglesias, Enrique. 2005. Farewell speech as President of the Inter-American Development Bank September 29, 2005. Washington, D.C.

Inman, Samuel Guy. 1965. "Inter-American Conferences, 1826-1954: History and Problems." University Press of Washington D.C. and the Community College Press. Washington D.C.

International American Conference (1st: 1889-90: Washington, D.C.). Volume: 2. http://www.archive.org/details/reportsofcommitt02interich

Inter-American Conference on Problems of War and Peace. 1945. Inter-American Reciprocal Assistance and Solidarity Resolution (Act of Chapultepec). http://avalon.law.yale.edu/20th_century/chapul.asp

Inter-American Development Bank. 2001. "40 Years: More than a Bank." Inter-American Development Bank, Washington, D.C.

Inter-American Development Bank. 2006. "Al Servicio de algo más que un Banco: Enrique V. Iglesias, presidente del BID (1988-2005)." Inter-American Development Bank, Washington, D.C.

Jackson, Donald. 1954. "Special Study Mission to Latin America on Technical Cooperation." Report by Rep. Donald L. Jackson, Subcommittee Chairman. Committee on Foreign Affairs, House. 1954.

John Paul II (1987) "Sollicitudo Rei Socialis" ("The Social Concern of the Church")
December 30, 1987 [Issued February 19, 1988].
http://www.vatican.va/edocs/ENG0223/_INDEX.HTM

Kapur, D., J. P. Lewis, and R. Webb. 1997. "The World Bank: its first half century." Volume I: History. Brookings Institution, Washington, D.C.

Kaufman, Burton. 1971. "United States Trade and Latin America: The Wilson Years." The Journal of American History, Vol. 58, No. 2, September, pp. 342-363.

Kirby, Maurice W. 1981. "The Decline of British Economic Power since 1870." London ; Boston : Allen & Unwin, 1981.

Krasner, Stephen. 1981. "Power Structures and Regional Development Banks." International Organization, Vol. 35, No. 2, Spring, pp. 303-328.

Maddison, Angus, 2003. "The World Economy: Historical Statistics." Development Centre of the Organization for Economic Cooperation and Development, OECD, Development Centre Studies, Paris.

Maisch, Christian. 2004. "Free Trade—The Inter-American System's Oldest and Newest Goal: The Evolution of Economic Themes in Inter-American Relations from the 1800s to the Present." In Middle Atlantic Council of Latin American Studies (MACLAS), Latin American Essays, Volume XVII. Available at http://maclas.org/pages/journal/essays-xvii/essays-xvii-christian-j.-maisch.php

Martí, José. 1891. "The Monetary Conference of the American Republics" http://www.cubaminrex.cu/english/NationalHeroe/Articulos/Diplomat/The-Monetary.html

Mason, E.S, and R. E. Asher. 1973. "The World Bank Since Bretton Woods." Brookings Institution, Washington, D.C.

McKinsey Global Institute. 2010. "Farewell to cheap capital? The Implications of long-term shifts in global investment and saving." December 2010. http://www.mckinsey.com/mgi/publications/farewell_cheap_capital/pdfs/MGI_Farewell_to_cheap_capital_full_report.pdf

The New York Times. 1898. "Populist Day in the House." December 18, 1898. Available at http://query.nytimes.com/mem/archive-free/pdf?res=9907E7D81030E333A2575BC1A9649D94699ED7CF

Nyhart, Joseph. 1968. "Development Banking: Global Patterns." Working Paper, Sloan School of Management, August 1968.

Organization of American States. 1954. "Declaration of Solidarity at the Tenth Conference of American States in Caracas." Available at http://avalon.law.yale.edu/20th_century/intam10.asp

Osgood, Robert. 1953. "Ideals and Self-Interest in America's Foreign Relations" University of Chicago Press. June 1953

Peskin, Allan. 1979. "Blaine, Garfield and Latin America: A New Look." The Americas, Vol. 36, No. 1, July, pp. 79-89 Published by: Catholic University of America Press on behalf of Academy of American Franciscan History.

Pletcher, David M. 1978. "Reciprocity and Latin America in the Early 1890s: A Foretaste of Dollar Diplomacy." The Pacific Historical Review, Vol. 47, No. 1, February, pp. 53-89.

Polity IV. 2009. Polity IV Country Reports. Available at http://www.systemicpeace.org/polity/polity06.htm#nam

Proceedings of the First Pan-American Financial Conference. 1915. Government Printing Office, Washington D.C., pp. 11. Available at http://www.archive.org/stream/proceedingsoffir00panarich#page/n5/mode/2up

Rabe, Stephen. 1988. "Eisenhower and Latin America: the foreign policy of anticommunism." University of North Carolina Press, Chapel Hill.

"Randall Commission" The President's Commission on Foreign Economic Policy. Report to the President and the Congress. 1954. Washington D.C. Government Printing Office.

Rees, David. 1973. "Harry Dexter White: a Study in Paradox." Coward, McCann & Geoghegan, New York, NY.

Roosevelt, Theodore. 1904 State of the Union. 1904. Address to the congress by President Theodore Roosevelt. Available at http://www.theodore-roosevelt.com/images/research/speeches/sotu4.pdf

Schlesinger, Arthur M. Jr. 1965. "A thousand days: John F. Kennedy in the White House." Houghton Mifflin Company, Boston M.A. and The Riverside Press, Cambridge M.A.

Schlesinger, Stephen. 2003. "The Act of Creation: The Founding of the United Nations." Westview Press, Cambridge, M.A..

Schwartz, Anna. 2001. "IMF's Origins as a Blueprint for its future." NBER, Lecture Series, November 5. Available at: http://web.gc.cuny.edu/eusc/activities/paper/schwartz.htm

Smith, Peter. 1996. "Talons of the Eagle: Dynamics of U.S.-Latin American Relations." Oxford University Press.

Stern, Nicholas. 2006. "Stern Review Report on the Economics of Climate Change." Available at http://www.hm-treasury.gov.uk/stern_review_report.htm

Third International American Conference, Río de Janeiro. 1906. Acts, resolutions and documents. Report of the Delegates of the United States: pp. 136.

Available at
http://www.archive.org/stream/cu31924021183573#page/n5/mode/2up

Thorp, Rosemary. 1992. "A reappraisal of the origins of import substituting industrialization 1930-1950." Journal of Latin American Studies, Vol. 24.

Thorp, Rosemary. 1998. "Progress, Poverty and Exclusion: an economic history of Latin America in the 20th century." Inter-American Development Bank, Washington, D.C.

Time Magazine. 1958. "Priority Begins at Home." Published on October 6. Available at;
http://www.time.com/time/magazine/article/0,9171,825508,00.html

Time Magazine. 1964. "The Alianza: Our Bank." Published on April 24. Available at
http://www.time.com/time/magazine/article/0,9171,870882,00.html

Tomassini, Luciano. 1997. "Felipe Herrera: a biographical essay." Inter-American Development Bank, Washington, D.C.

Trussell, C.R. 1959. "Congress Backs A Latin-Aid Bank: Passes Bill Approving U.S. Role in New Billion-Dollar Development Agency." Published on The New York Times on July 28, pp. 1.

U.S. House of Representatives. 1890. Committee on Banking and Currency. Report on the International American Bank. 51th Congress, June 26, 1890. Report 2561 to accompany H.R. 11159

U.S. House of Representatives. 1892. Committee on Banking and Currency. Report on the International American Bank. 52th Congress, April 5, 1892. Report 985 to accompany H.R. 7885.

U.S. House of Representatives. 1897. Committee on Banking and Currency. Report on the International American Bank. 52th Congress, February27, 1897. Report 3054 to accompany H.R. 875.

U.S. House of Representatives. 1959. Committee on Banking and Currency. 86th Congress, 1st Session, July 16, 1959. Report No. 678.

U.S. Senate. 1941. Hearings before a Subcommittee of the Committee on Foreign Relations United State Senate: A Convention for the Establishment of an Inter-American Bank, signed on behalf of the, United States of America on May, 1940. May 5 and 6, United States Government Printing Office, Washington D.C. 1941

U.S. Senate. 1959. Senate Report No. 86-487 to Accompany S. 1928, 86th Congress, 1st Session, P.L. 86-147, July 8.

Villaseñor, Eduardo. 1941. "The Inter-American Bank: Prospects and Dangers." Foreign Affairs, 20(1), pp. 165-174.

Villaseñor, Eduardo. 1948. "El Banco Interamericano." El Trimestre Económico, Fondo de Cultura Económica, México, pp. 177-193.

Washington, George. 1796. Washington's Farewell Address 1796. The Avalon Project. Available at http://avalon.law.yale.edu/18th_century/washing.asp

The Washington Post. 1930. "Pan-American Farm Bank." Published on September 24 pp. 6.

The Washington Post. 1939. "Subcommittee Proposes Bank for Americas." Published on November 24, pp. 11.

Wilson, T.A., and R. McKinzie. 1971. Oral History Interview with Emilio Collado. New York, July 7.

Wilson, W. State of the Union. 1914. Address to the congress by President Woodrow Wilson. Available at http://www.presidency.ucsb.edu/ws/index.php?pid=29555

Index

"Good Neighbor" policy, 30
"New Freedom" program, 16
1864 Congress in Lima, Perú, 2
1930 Pan-American Agricultural Conference, 26
1955 Santiago proposal, 71
1956 Meeting of the presidents of the Americas, 62
1957 OAS Economic Conference, 62, 63
Acheson, Dean, 43
African Development Bank, 102, 103, 107
Alberdi, Juan Bautista, 1
Allende, Salvador, 84
Alliance for Progress, xv, 65, 75, 77, 79, 80, 84, 91, 93, 110, 111
American League of Nations, 21
Anderson, Robert, 64
Arab development institution, 68, 69
Arbenz, Jacobo, 55
Asian Development Bank, 102, 103, 107
Baring Bank crisis, 89
Berle, A.A., 37
Birdsall, Nancy, 82
Black, Eugene, 71, 72, 81
Blaine, James, 3, 4
Board of Executive Directors, 73, 111, 137
Board of Governors, 34, 73, 122
Bogotá Act, 77, 79, 80, 84
Bolívar, Simón, 1, 62

Bretton Woods Conference, 1944, 39, 44, 45
Bretton Woods Institutions, 41, 46, 49, 63, 76, 110, 112
British Abnormal Importations Act, 25
British Commonwealth Preferences, 25
Brosius, Marriott, 8
Bureau of American Republics, 15
Bush, George H.W., 94, 95
Bush, George W., 95, 112
Cabot, John Moors, 53
Cafiero, Antonio, 57
Callable capital, 72, 106, 109
Calvo Doctrine, 14
Cancún, 114
Capital increase, 92, 98, 106, 108, 112
Caribbean Development Bank, 94
CARICOM, 94
Cartagena Treaty, 94
Castro, Fidel, 69, 77
Central American Bank of Economic Integration, 94
Central American Common Market, 94
Chapultepec Act, 45
Charter of Punta del Este, 79, 120
Chester, Arthur, 4
Citizen security, 115
Clay, Henry, 2
Clinton Administration, 95, 112

Cold War, xv, 46, 47, 48, 64, 77, 84, 92, 119

Collado, Emilio, 37, 42, 120, 127

Commercial Bureau of the American Republics, 9

Committee of Experts Meeting, Santiago, 1955, 58, 111

Communist Party Congress of 1956, 64

Conference for the Maintenance of Continental Peace and Security, Rio de Janeiro, 1947, 48

Corporación Andina de Fomento, 94

Corporaciones de Fomento, 46

Debt crisis of the 1980s, 94

Debtors' bank, xi, 76

Declaration of Punta del Este, 1961, 80, 93, 120

Declaration of Solidarity for the Preservation of the Political Integrity of the American States against International Communist Intervention, 53

Democracy, 30, 48, 50, 51, 65, 67, 68, 79, 83, 87, 88, 94, 107, 109, 114

Dexter, White Harry, 30, 33, 34, 125

Dillon, Clarence Douglas, xi, 64, 66, 68, 69, 75, 77

Drago Doctrine, 14

Drago, Luis María, 14

Dulles, John Foster, 53, 67, 70

Economic Charter of the Americas, 49

Economic Commission of Latin America and the Caribbean (ECLAC), 50, 93, 95

Economic Declaration of Buenos Aires, 64

Economic shocks of the mid-1970s, 94

Eighth Capital Increase, 27, 30, 92

Eighth Inter-American Conference, Lima, 1938, 27, 30

Eisenhower Administration, xv, 52, 53, 55, 58, 62, 63, 64, 65, 66, 70, 77, 80, 81, 84, 102, 110

Eisenhower Doctrine, 63

Eisenhower, Dwight, 121

Eisenhower, Milton, 53, 64, 66, 68

Enterprise for the Americas Initiative, 94

European Economic Community, 63

European Union, xvi, 96, 97, 101

Exchange controls, 30, 40

Exchange rates, 10, 11, 15, 19, 20, 21, 37, 43, 90, 93

Exchange Stabilization Fund, 28, 29, 43, 119

Export-Import Bank, 28, 30, 32, 38, 39, 45, 49, 50, 53, 55, 56, 57, 63, 75

Fascism, 84

FDR Administration, xiv, 29

Federal Reserve, 7, 8, 16, 17, 18, 19, 20, 23, 34, 37, 39, 40, 90, 122

Financial rating, 109

Financial Times, 113

First American Congress, Panama, 1, 93

First IDB loan, 81

First Meeting of Consultation of Foreign Ministers of the American Republics, Panama, 1939, 32

First Meeting of Finance Ministers of the American Republics, Guatemala, 1939, 33

First Meeting of Governors of the IDB, San Salvador, 1960, 77

First National City Bank of New York, 17

First Pan-American Conference, Washington D.C., 1889-1890., 15, 17

First Pan-American Financial Conference, Washington D.C., 1915, xiv, 4, 19, 125

Fourth Pan-American Commercial Conference, Washington D.C., 1931, 26

Fourth Pan-American Conference, Buenos Aires, 1910, 15

Franco, Francisco, 29

Free Trade Agreement of the Americas, 94, 95

Frei, Eduardo, 56

Frondizi, Arturo, 65, 67, 78

Fund for Special Operations (FSO), 37, 71, 72, 98, 112

G-20, xvi

García, Enrique, 114

Garfield, James, 3, 4, 124

General Agreement on Tariffs and Trade (GATT), 27, 47

Glass, Carter, 16, 40

Glass-Steagall Act, 40

Gold Clearance Fund Convention, 20, 21, 43, 90

Gold Reserve Act, 28

Gold standard, 15, 17, 20, 21, 22, 90

Great Depression, xiv, 23, 25, 27, 30, 47, 90

Hague Convention of 1899, 13

Harding Administration, 20, 21

Harrison, Benjamin, 4

Henderson, John 9

Herrera, Felipe, vii, x, xi, 57, 76, 77, 81, 82, 85, 91, 93, 113, 126, 135

Holland, Henry, 66

House, Edward ("Colonel"), 18

House of Representatives, 8, 9, 10, 75, 126

Hull, Cordell, 28

Humphrey, George, 55, 57, 58, 64

Iglesias, Enrique, vii, x, 81, 87, 92, 94, 105, 113

Illia Administration, 94

Imbalances in the global economy, 96, 99

Institute for Latin American Integration (INTAL), 94

Inter-American Agricultural Bank, 26

Inter-American Bank (I-AB), xiv, 20, 25, 27, 32, 34, 37, 38, 41, 46, 50, 60, 61, 71, 84, 90, 93, 101, 110, 122, 126, 127

Inter-American Conference for the Maintenance of Peace, Buenos Aires, 1936, 29

Inter-American Conference on Problems of War and Peace, Mexico, 1945, 48, 123

Inter-American Development Bank (IDB), vii, x, xi, xiii, xv, 37, 38, 39, 47, 52, 59, 69, 70, 71, 72, 74, 77, 82, 83, 98, 101, 102, 103, 104, 109, 112, 114, 120, 122, 123, 126, 135, 137

Inter-American Economic and Financial Institute, 30

Inter-American Economic and Social Council (CIES), 20, 49, 61, 64, 70

Inter-American Financial and Economic Advisory Committee (IAFEAC), 20, 33

Inter-American Fund for the Development of Industry, Agriculture, and Mining, 56

Inter-American High Commission
(IAHC), 20, 119
Inter-American Reciprocal
Assistance and Solidarity Act,
48
International American Bank, xiv,
1, 4, 5, 6, 7, 8, 9, 10, 13, 16, 17,
22, 71, 84, 89, 90, 101, 126
International American Monetary
Commission, 10
International Bank for
Reconstruction and
Development, 43
International Bureau of American
Republics, 14
International Development
Association, 72
International Finance Corporation,
56
International High Commission,
19, 119
International investment, 15
International Monetary Fund
(IMF), xiv, 20, 39, 43, 90, 119,
122
Jefferson, Thomas, 2, 86
John Paul II, 116
Kennedy Administration, 80, 81,
110
Kennedy, John F., 79, 107
Korean War, 54, 90
Kubitschek, Juscelino, 66, 67, 78,
111, 121
Lansing, Robert, 18
Latin American Free Trade
Association, 94
League of Nations, 18, 44, 110
Lebanon, 68
Lleras Camargo, Alberto, 55
Lleras Restrepo, Carlos, 56
Maddison, Angus, xiii
Managua Treaty, 94
Manifest Destiny, 2

Marshall Plan, 47, 52
Mc Adoo, William, 18
McCloy, John, 50, 71
MERCOSUR, 94
Mexican War, 2
Mikesell, Raymond, 59
Monroe Doctrine, xiii, 2, 3, 4, 26
Monroney, Mike, 71
Moreno, Luis Alberto, 88
Morgenthau, Henry, 28, 30, 31
Multilateral Debt Relief Initiative,
105
Multilateral Investment Fund, 115
Mussolini, Benito, 26
National Advisory Committee on
Inter-American Affairs, 77
National City Bank of New York,
39
Nazism, 29, 84
New Deal, 52
Ninth Capital increase, 92, 98,
100, 106, 108
Ninth Inter-American Conference,
Bogotá, 1948, 49
Nitze, Paul, 51
Nixon Administration, 84, 111
Nixon, Richard, 58, 110
NSC 68, 51
OAS charter, 63
Oil shock in the 1970s, 114
Operation Pan-America, 78
Ordinary Capital, 71, 72, 75, 80,
81, 98, 102, 103, 106, 108, 112
Organization of American States,
20
Organization of American States
(OAS), 9, 14, 49, 53, 57, 69,
124, 137
Ortiz Mena, Antonio, 85, 92, 112
Ottawa Conference, 28
Owen, Robert L., 16
Pan-American Economic Agency,
26

Pan-American Union, 9, 15, 30, 37, 49

Pérez Jiménez, Marcos, 66

Prebisch, Raúl, 49, 51, 54, 56, 58, 70, 77, 80, 93, 111, 121

Proposal for a gold fund, 20

Quitandinha Meeting, Rio de Janeiro, 1954, 55, 64

Reagan Administration, 85

Reciprocity agreements, 10

Redfield, William, 18

Rio Treaty, 48, 63, 110

Rockefeller, Nelson, 45

Roosevelt [Theodore] Corollary, 14

Roosevelt, Franklin Delano, 26

Roosevelt Theodore, 3, 14, 26, 125

Roosevelt's [Theodore] Doctrine, 3

Root, Elihu, 15

Rubottom, Roy, 68

Saenz Peña, Roque, 9

Second Bank of the United States, 16

Second International Conference, The Hague, 1907, 15

Second Pan-American Conference, Mexico, 1901-1902, 13

Second Pan-American Financial Conference, Washington D.C., 1920, 20

Second Pan-American Scientific Congress, Washington D.C., 1916, 18

Security Council, 44, 68

Seventh Capital increase, 26, 27, 92, 111, 112

Seventh Inter-American Conference, Montevideo, 1933, 27

Sixth Pan-American Conference, La Havana, 1928, 21

Smoot-Hawley Tariff, 25, 28

Social Progress Trust Fund, 78, 80

Summit of the Americas in Mar del Plata, 2005, 95, 100

Taft, Robert, 39

Technical cooperation, 50, 75, 84

The Bankers Magazine, 20, 119

Third Conference of Ministers of Foreign Relations, Rio de Janeiro, 1942, 41

Third Pan-American Conference, Rio de Janeiro, 1906, 14

Third Reich, 26

Treaty of Rome, 1957, 63

Treaty on Inter-American Trade Liberalization and Economic Non-Aggression, 30

Truman Administration, xv, 51, 52, 53

Truman Doctrine, 47

Truman, Harry S., 120

Truman's Point Four, 51

U.N. Charter, 45

U.N. Conference in San Francisco, 1948, 48

U.N. Economic and Employment Commission, 71

U.S. Civil War, 2

Underwood-Simmons Act, 16

United Nations (U.N.), 43, 44, 48, 49, 68, 69, 121, 125, 137

United States, ix, xi, xii, xiii, xv, xvi, 1, 2, 3, 4, 5, 6, 7, 8, 9, 10, 11, 13, 14, 16, 17, 18, 19, 21, 22, 25, 26, 27, 28, 29, 30, 31, 32, 33, 34, 35, 36, 37, 38, 39, 41, 43, 44, 45, 47, 49, 50, 51, 53, 54, 55, 56, 57, 58, 60, 62, 63, 64, 65, 66, 69, 70, 72, 74, 76,78, 79, 81, 84, 86, 89, 90, 91, 96, 97, 100, 101, 102, 104, 105, 106, 107, 108, 110, 111,

112, 113, 123, 125, 126, 135, 137

Upton, T. Graydon, 75

Vanderberg, Arthur H., 45

Venezuelan Fund, 114

Villaseñor, Eduardo 34, 39, 41, 44, 60, 92, 127

Washington, George, vii, 2

Washington Post, 26, 36, 39, 127

Welles, Benjamin Sumner, 32, 34, 37, 44

Wilson Administration, 16, 20, 44

Wilson, Woodrow, 16, 17, 18, 44, 110, 127

World Bank, xi, xiv, 38, 39, 42, 43, 50, 56, 57, 61, 71, 75, 76, 80, 81, 90, 92, 103, 107, 112, 113, 116, 119, 123, 124, 137

World War I (WWI), xiv, 17, 19, 21, 90, 110

World War II (WWII), xiv, 25, 30, 31, 33, 41, 45, 47, 48, 49, 55, 65, 110

Back Cover

At the 1964 annual meeting of the Inter-American Development Bank (IDB) in Panama, Felipe Herrera, then the President of the institution, argued that "our institution must continue to demonstrate that, being a bank, it is also more than a bank...."

What is this institution that had the backing of both Latin American countries and the United States, and that since Herrera many have claimed it is "more than a bank"? And how did it come into existence?

Although the IDB was formally established in 1959, the long and complex historical journey leading to its creation started far earlier in the nineteenth century. Now that the IDB has passed the threshold of fifty years since its formal creation it may be the right time to look at the rich institutional history of the Bank and to think about its future.

Also, a better understanding of the emergence and evolution of the IDB can contribute to the debate about how to build more adequate structures of international governance – a key issue now that deficits in global policy-making are constraining the functioning of the world economy.

The Authors

Eugenio Díaz Bonilla is an economist with more than thirty years of professional experience in development issues. He has been a consultant and staff member with several international organizations: World Bank, United Nations Development Program (UNDP), Food and Agriculture Organization (FAO), Inter-American Institute for Cooperation in Agriculture (IICA), Organization of American States (OAS), and the International Food Policy Research Institute (IFPRI). He worked as senior advisor to Ministers and public officials in different developing countries and has also held diplomatic positions for his country, Argentina, working on agricultural trade negotiations. He has been member of the Board of Executive Directors of the Inter-American Development Bank (IADB) since 2003. Mr. Díaz Bonilla has published extensively on poverty, food security, trade and macroeconomic issues in developing countries and has taught in Universities in Latin America and the United States. He graduated as Licenciado en Economía of the Universidad de Buenos Aires (Argentina), and holds a Master of Arts in International Relations from the School of Advanced International Studies, and a Ph.D. in Economics, both from The Johns Hopkins University (USA).

Maria Victoria del Campo is a Ph.D. candidate at the Massachusetts Institute of Technology's International Development Group. She has worked for the office of the representatives for Argentina and Haiti at the Board of Executive Directors of the IDB. Ms. del Campo holds a MA in Economic Development from Nagoya University (Japan), and a BA in International Relations from the University of Tsukuba (Japan).